A JEW IN THE NEW GERMANY

# the
# humanities
# laboratory

# A Jew in the New Germany

**HENRYK BRODER**

Translated from the German
by the Broder Translators' Collective

Edited by Sander L. Gilman
and Lilian M. Friedberg

UNIVERSITY OF
ILLINOIS PRESS

URBANA AND
CHICAGO

Library of Congress
Cataloging-in-Publication Data
Broder, Henryk M., 1946–
A Jew in the new Germany /
Henryk Broder ;
translated from the German by the
Broder Translators' Collective ;
edited by Sander L. Gilman
and Lilian M. Friedberg.
p.   cm. – (Humanities laboratory)
ISBN 0-252-02856-2 (cloth : alk.
paper)
1. Jews–Germany–Identity.
2. Jews–Cultural assimilation–
Germany. 3. Jews–Germany–
Social conditions–20th century.
4. Germany–Social conditions–20th
century. 5. Germany–Ethnic relations.
I. Gilman, Sander L. II. Friedberg,
Lilian M. III. Title. IV. Series.
DS135.G332B76      2004
305.892'4043'09045—DC21
2002153958

# Contents

# Acknowledgments

The essays collected in *A Jew in the New Germany* were first published in German and appeared in the following publications:

"Warum ich lieber kein Jude wäre; und wenn schon unbedingt–dann lieber nicht in Deutschland," in *Fremd im eigenen Land: Juden in der Bundesrepublik* by Henryk Broder. Frankfurt a.M.: Fischer Taschenbuch Verlag, 1979. 82–102.

"Ihr bleibt die Kinder eurer Eltern: Die neue deutsche Linke und der alltägliche Antisemitismus" and "Warum ich gehe," *Zeit-Forum* 27 (February 1981): 243–60.

"Heimat? Nein danke!" in *Ich liebe Karstadt, und andere Lobreden* by Henryk Broder. Augsburg: Ölbaum Verlag, 1987. 7–14, 36–37.

"Und das Differenzieren nicht vergessen," in *Ich liebe Karstadt, und andere Lobreden,* 133–36.

"Ich liebe Karstadt," in *Ich liebe Karstadt, und andere Lobreden,* 185–204.

"Unser Kampf," *Der Spiegel* 31 (January 1991): 170–85.

"Deutsche unter sich," in *Erbarmen mit den Deutschen* by Henryk Broder. Hamburg: Hoffman and Campe, 1994. 15–20.

"Eine schöne Revolution," in *Erbarmen mit den Deutschen,* 21–24.

"Die Republik der Simulanten," in *Erbarmen mit den Deutschen,* 47–54.

"Ratlose Aufklärer," in *Schöne Bescherung! Unterwegs im neuen Deutschland* by Henryk Broder. Augsburg: Ölbaum Verlag, 1994. 95–99.

"Ostalgie: Die DDR ist wieder da," in *Volk und Wahn* by Henryk Broder. Berlin: Goldmann Verlag, 1996. 35–48.

"Germanisierung des Holocausts," in *Volk und Wahn,* 214–28.

"Problem, Schock, und Trauma," in *Die Irren von Zion* by Henryk Broder. Hamburg: Hoffman and Campe, 1998. 21–27.

"Wer kämpft ist noch nicht tot," in *Die Irren von Zion*, 251–55.

"Tagar and die Tipi-Familie," in *Die Irren von Zion*, 115–27.

"Jedem das Seine," in *Jedem das Seine* by Henryk Broder. Augsburg: Ölbaum Verlag, 1999. 7–9.

"Jedem sein Marktwert," in *Jedem das Seine*, 21–29.

"Just in Time: Der Moraltheologe an der Terrorfront," in *Kein Krieg, Nirgends: Die Deutschen und der Terror* by Henryk Broder. Berlin: Verlag, 2002. 15–26.

# Introduction

SANDER L. GILMAN

There is a public literary tradition in German writing that can be called "caustic cultural commentary." It is a type of essayistic writing written for the general public that has civic betterment as its goal and satire as its literary tool. Often as not appearing in the form of the feuilleton, the newspaper essay, it forms a rather special German tradition. There was virtually no other public space for critical debates in German from the Enlightenment through the founding of the Federal Republic in 1949, with the exception of the very small window of the Weimar Republic from 1919 to 1933. There was neither a tradition of parliamentary oratory nor an understanding of a public sphere in which ideas could be exchanged with any expectation that the debate would actually impact public action. The feuilleton is the important exception to the absence of this democratic tradition in Germany. As is typical of such literary forms that provided a minimal space in the public sphere in Germany, the feuilleton was created in Paris when Julien-Louis Geoffroy, the drama critic for the *Journal des Débats*, began publishing them in 1800.

From the Prussian Enlightenment to the Nazi Reich, the authors of such critical feuilleton texts were exiled, prosecuted, and occasionally murdered–the most notable modern case being Carl von Ossietzky, who was arrested by the Nazis on February 28, 1933, the morning after the Reichstag fire. He was initially sent to a Berlin prison and then on to concentration camps–Sonnenburg and later to Esterwegen-Papenburg–where, according to reports from fellow prisoners, he was badly mistreated. He was awarded the Nobel Peace Prize in 1936 for his vehement feuilletons in opposition to the Nazis and to all of those forces opposed to the idea of a democracy. He died in 1938 as a result of his injuries in the concentration camps.

Those who were not beaten or killed still seemed always to live on the margins. Heinrich Heine and Ludwig Börne both wrote their critical feuilletons from mid-nineteenth-century Paris, where Théophile Gautier and Charles-Augustin Sainte-Beuve were also honing the form. In late nineteenth-century and early twentieth-century Vienna, Friedrich Kürenberg, Eduard Hanslick, Daniel Spitzer (Freud's favorite), Karl Kraus, and Felix Salten sharpened and focused the feuilleton; for them it provided a public forum for critical debates in politics, literature, and music in the Imperial Monarchy and beyond. In Berlin, Theodor Fontane and Moriz Saphir became the acknowledged masters of the form. What is remarkable in all of them is the tone: often satiric or ironic, sometimes lightly pricking the pomposity of the cultural or political elite, sometimes attacking them ferociously, without giving quarter. Always aware of the reading public in their pedagogical turn, the authors of feuilletons saw their job as not only to enlighten their readers but also to move them to action.

If there was a "high point" of this tradition in Germany and Austria it was in the 1920s. From the intellectuals of the Romanische Café in Berlin to those sitting in the Café Central in Vienna, all seemed to write feuilletons. By 1930, in Berlin alone there were 147 newspapers in which they were published. Hermann Hesse spoke of a "feuilletonistic age," but he did not mean this as a compliment. From Kurt Tucholsky on the radical Left to "Rumpelstilzchen" (Adolf Stein) on the ultraconservative Right, the articles "below the line" were featured on the front pages and read by everyone—they were literally below the line that divided the "news hole" from the feuilleton. "Serious" writers like Hesse thought the practice smacked too much of journalism, which, of course, it did. After the founding of German democracy in 1949, this tradition remained a rich vein of criticism that often goaded politicians, who themselves were uncomfortable with true public opposition, into democratic directions.

What is most confounding about this tradition is that virtually all of its greatest exponents seemed to have been Jews. From Ludwig Börne to Heinrich Heine, Daniel Spitzer, Moriz Saphir, Peter Altenberg, Karl Kraus, Alfred Polgar, Walter Kerr, Egon Friedell, Felix Salten, Kurt Tucholsky, Egon Erwin Kisch, and Robert Neumann, all were publicly identified as Jews. It was of little consequence if (like Heine) they had converted to Christianity or (like Tucholsky) they were Communists and atheists. And in virtually all of the cases listed above, the "Jewishness" of the authors was a marginal part of their own consciousness, except when the term was used as a weapon to attack them. They were identified as Jews as much by their caustic voices demanding change from the status quo as by anything else.

Since Jews were seen as not truly belonging to the countries they lived in, they became associated with such critical views because, presumably, only outsiders to the political system could assume these ideological positions. Few Jews held posts in the government. Jews were the "pariah nation" of outsiders who forced change in their adopted homelands (at least according to the dean of modern sociologists, Max Weber). Now this view of Jewish intellectuals and journalists (not always the same thing) seemed to be commonplace even though some of Weber's Jewish contemporaries like Albert Norden or Gerson von Bleichröder were the epitome of the Wilhelmenian "insider." The irony is that the tradition of caustic civil critique became labeled as "Jewish" in a cycle of labeling and counterlabeling and that Jews came to be identified as its creators or exponents, whether they were (Heine) or were not (von Ossietzky) Jewish. It is true that journalism was one of the "free professions" where one could function without state certification or social status. As a result, Jews (no matter what their beliefs) were overrepresented in the profession by the middle of the nineteenth century, or at least writers as early as Gustav Freytag (in his 1854 comedy *The Journalists*) thought them to be. But the claim that Jews dominated the world of the feuilleton holds a kernel of truth. Often it was indeed "Jews" (no matter how defined), sensing themselves on the margins or placing themselves self-consciously on the margins of "polite" discourse, who mastered this medium. And yet it was also an "insider's" medium in that a feuilletonist could write as a freelancer but still needed to be published, preferably in daily newspapers or mass circulation magazines to reach the broadest audience.

Under the Nazi regime, this critical voice was lost with the onset of state-controlled publications. The destruction of much of German Jewry robbed the German press of many of its most notable feuilleton writers. By the founding of the Federal Republic of Germany (FRG) and the German Democratic Republic (GDR) in 1949, the tradition of the German Jewish feuilleton seemed to have vanished. The feuilleton, of course, reappeared, but there were virtually no "Jewish" voices to be heard. While some Weimar writers such as Robert Neumann reappeared on the German scene after 1949, no young critical "Jewish" voice was heard in German until the beginning of the student revolts in the 1960s. This was equally true in West and East Germany, where the feuilletonist was reborn as hack supporter of the "official" party position on all issues. The critical voice so long associated with the "Jewish" feuilletonist reappeared with the writing of the Polish-born essayist Henryk Broder. Inspired by his public role, this tradition has now continued in a different public form in the twenty-first century with the next generation of German Jews, such as Maxim Biller and Wladmir Kaminer, and more recently with the politician-turned-talk-show-host Michel Friedmann. The irony is that these examples of the next generation to have picked up the torch from Broder were born in Czechoslovakia, the Soviet Union, and France, respectively.

Broder's importance as a link in this chain of satirical public commentary cannot be underestimated. His voice came to be more and more the voice of the German Jewish counterculture. Not the official and often self-consciously invisible role of the Jewish community, always serious and often pathetic, Broder positioned himself early on as a public gadfly. Like many German Jews today (if not most of those engaged in the critical public sphere, such as those mentioned above), Broder was not born in Germany. He was an Eastern European Jew. Born on August 20, 1946, in Katowice, Poland, his parents—his mother Felicja, who died in 1995 at the age of ninety, and his father Kalman, who died in 1976 at the age of eighty-one—had survived the camps. A Polish Catholic family hid his older sister Janina, born in 1937 in Krakow, as a "Catholic" child from 1941 until 1945. Today she lives in Paris.

The Poland that the Broder family lived in after 1945 seemed to have not seen enough killing of Jews before 1945, some of it carried out by Poles murdering their Jewish neighbors.[1] In July 1946 in Kielce, south of Warsaw, a town that had fifty thousand inhabitants and 350 Jews (down from twenty-five thousand in 1939), there was a pogrom. Spurred by the spread of the ancient blood libel (that Jews had slaughtered Christian children for their blood), Poles murdered forty-two Jews, including women and children. By April 1946 alone, over a thousand Jews had been murdered in Poland. A doctor who fled Lodz stated: "'The government is 100 percent for us; the people 100 percent against us.'"[2] Gitta Guttmann returned to a small town near Lodz in 1946: "'It was a horrible experience. The only good thing was that I found my mother. . . . It was a huge cemetery. I became so sick. Not that I had any physical symptoms like fever. I was psychologically ill. I was sick for weeks. Simply could not understand what had happened.'"[3] The idea of remaining in Poland, a country that before 1939 had betrayed them by offering and then rescinding their identity as Polish Jews, and which continued to betray them after 1945, was difficult for Broder's parents.

Yet they, like many Polish Jews (such as the critic Marcel Reich-Ranicki, among others), remained in Poland until the second wave of anti-Semitism began to drive the remnants of the Jews out of Communist Poland. After the show trial of the "Jew" Rudolph Slansky in 1952 in Prague and the aftershocks of the so-called Jewish doctors' plot against Stalin in 1953, being Jewish or even of Jewish ancestry was not necessarily seen as positive in the East Block. In Poland the attacks on Zionism and crypto-Zionists made life for the Jews of Poland, many of whom had strongly identified with the new Communist state, untenable. It compromised the very idea of a Jewish identity in the East Block.[4] Even after Stalin's death these attacks increased. In 1957 the Broder family moved from Poland to Vienna and the next year from Vienna to Cologne. It was in Vienna that the Polish-speaking ten-year-old Henryk began to learn German. He hung out at the Naschmarkt, the public market in the center of the old city where he listened and learned to pick up the ironic tone that lay beneath the extreme politeness of the Viennese. In this sense he began, quite unconsciously, to follow in the footsteps of other Eastern European Jews, such as Felix Salten, who came to Vienna to polish their German and learn to write feuilletons. Salten, best known as the author of *Bambi*, was mocked by his Viennese counterpart Karl Kraus in his own feuilletons for revealing his provincial background in everything he wrote. Broder would not fall into the same trap.

It was in Cologne that Henryk formally attended school, receiving his Abitur from the Hansa-Gymnasium there in 1966. Now a "German" by language and culture, he nevertheless remained identified as an outsider in being a Polish Jew. As a student he began writing for the high school newspaper. After completing his Abitur he began to freelance for the West German Radio (WDR), the liberal newspaper, the *Frankfurter Rundschau*, as well as the DGB magazines of the German Workers' Union. Never wanting especially to be seen as a "Jewish" writer, Broder wrote on whatever topics were requested. He used this experience to begin honing his own special voice. Soon he was writing for such mass-market publications as the weekly liberal newspaper *Die Zeit*, the union paper *Welt der Arbeit*, as well as the satiric journals *konkret* and *Pardon*.

In 1981 Palestinian terrorists seized an El Al plane and forced it to land at Entebbe in Uganda. Sitting on the runway, the plane's passengers were eventually freed by the heroic intervention of Israeli Special Forces. Throughout the world this was heralded as an extraordinarily brave and risky action, especially with the death of the leader of the Israeli contingent, Jonathan Netanyahu. There was a contrary voice, however, and it was loudly heard in the Federal Republic of Germany on the German Left. Broder was appalled by the response of his "friends" on the Left who saw the rescue only as the thwarting of the legitimate demands of the Palestinians. In a blistering essay, "You Are Still Your Parents' Children: The New German Left and Everyday Anti-Semitism," he saw in their opposition a latent form of German anti-Semitism that he could no longer tolerate. Unable to live in Germany any longer he moved to Jerusalem and remained there for ten years. His final "blast" came in his collection of responses to young Jews in the Federal Republic of Germany, *A Stranger in My Own Country* (edited with Michel Lang in 1979). Broder was not alone. The Jewish novelist and short story writer Lea Fleischmann also left Germany for

Israel at that time, entitling her address to the Germans, *This Is Not My Country: A Jewess Leaves the Federal Republic* (1980). Both Broder and Fleischmann were strongly Zionist, but Broder's allegiance to Zionism retained the same type of skepticism that he felt in Germany. Indeed, by the 1990s, he was able to write a nuanced and differentiated book on the question of Israel and the Zionist project, *The Madmen of Zion*, written in German for a German audience. Even though he moved to Israel, he maintained his literary profile in Germany, continuing to write for major periodicals such as *Süddeutsche Zeitung, Profil, Weltwoche, Tagesanzeiger, Neue Zürcher,* and *Frankfurter Allgemeine Zeitung.* He developed a three-cornered identity, with "homes" in Augsburg, Jerusalem, and New York.

In the fall of 1990 he returned for a three- to four-month stay in Germany and then continued to live there, almost without public acknowledgment, on a permanent basis. (Lea Fleischmann remained in Israel but also continued to write popular books on Jewish topics for the German reading public.) He had a long-term relationship with Hilde Recher, who is not Jewish, and the couple had a daughter who was born in 1988. (They were finally married in 1999 and thus officially sealed a relationship that had continued even while Broder was in Israel.) Recher created the open Ölbaum Verlag in Augsburg in 1980, which is devoted to Jewish-oriented publications, including a number of her husband's books.

If the Entebbe Rescue caused Broder to rethink his position in regards to the German Left, the Gulf War in 1991 saw an ominous return of much of the same rhetoric. When it was revealed that the Iraqi war industry had used German chemists in manufacturing the arms with which it had massacred its own people, German capitalism seemed initially to be called into question. This the German Left loved. But when SCUD missiles rained down on Israel armed with that same poison gas, many German intellectuals of the Left saw this as the fault of the Israelis. What had been a war of aggression by Iraq against Kuwait was suddenly the result of Zionism's pernicious presence in the Middle East![5] Broder fulminated, and two weeks before the beginning of Operation Desert Storm he accused the German antiwar movement of having "difficulties with living Jews" in their seemingly compulsive "enthusiasm for dead Jews." In an essay that appeared in the liberal daily *taz* on January 2, 1991, Broder coined his most cited phrase: "Germans just love dead Jews–it's the living ones they can't handle." A man of the Left, Broder was more attuned than most of his contemporaries to the fine line that connected the anxiety and guilt about the Shoah with contemporary German anger at Israel for not being made in their image of what a "good" Jew should be.

In April 1995 Broder was appointed a regular correspondent for the major

German newsmagazine *Der Spiegel*, where he continues to write today. In 1997 he turned fifty. With his typical global and yet very local sensibility he spent his fiftieth birthday on Cape Cod, a citizen of the now global world of communications. Today, Broder is considered one of the most important commentators on political and cultural life in Germany as these relate to situations in other parts of the world–from the United States to Israel and the Middle East. Broder has produced and directed several documentary films (*The Jewish Cultural Association in Nazi Germany, 1933–1941; Yiddish Culture and Language in Israel;* and *Life and Death of Joseph Wulf*) and has authored an impressive array of books, many of which are collections of his journalistic writings. Recently he established a Web site (www.henryk-broder.com) where he publishes and collects his own work and keeps running polemics against a tradition of German cultural complacency. Whatever his venue, Broder consistently takes on the deeply troubling implications of the Holocaust for contemporary German life with great moral and analytical clarity.

After September 11, 2001, Broder was struck by a resurgence of precisely the "moral blindness" that caused him to leave Germany after Entebbe and the Gulf War. The German Left, as well as a large portion of the Left in Europe and the United States, suddenly saw 9/11 as a sign of the moral failure of the West! In Germany all of the old anti-Western clichés that had dominated the debates during the 1991 war against Iraq surfaced again. The "pop" philosophical guru Peter Sloterdijk, writing in the news magazine *Focus* on September 24, 2001, noted that "we have still not understood that Western democracy is the life form that is responsible for its own enemies–because they mirror its own political practice." And in a TV interview on November 4, 2001, the associate leader of the Liberal party (FDP) J. W. Möllemann placed the blame for 9/11 solidly on the shoulders of Israel's "politics of occupation." Not only were the actions of the terrorists on 9/11 the fault of the West's decadent imperialism, but it was the Jews who in some direct way were the catalyst for this action. If the rumors on the "Arab Street" had it that it was the Israeli secret service that destroyed the World Trade Center towers, then German intellectuals (among others) saw Zionism as the motor that drove the attack. Broder's answer to this is his most compelling book to date: *No War, No Where: The Germans and Terror* (2002).

The volume presented here is a representative sample of Broder's work spanning two decades and a wide array of topics. There is a wealth of stimulating material: from the debate over the construction of a Holocaust memorial in Berlin, to a view of the Gulf War from Germany, to Broder's personal ruminations on his own German Jewish identity. Of special note is Broder's insightful commentary on the politics of German reunification and his fierce criticisms of the totalitarian repression of the former GDR. The volume concludes with an extract from his book on the German responses to 9/11. Heedless of orthodoxies, Broder upsets the safe presumptions of both the political Right and Left about the basic tenets of life in a West Germany that claimed to have "worked through" its past and in an East Germany that claimed to have been based on fundamentally "antifascist" principles. Especially against the backdrop of the contemporary resurgence of Jewish culture in the Berlin Republic and the strife-ridden politics of post-unification nationalism, this collection of Broder's work fills a gap in American academic and public discourse with its refreshingly intelligent humor and mordant irony.

This volume is an example of the type of academic collaboration that, we hope, will mark the future of the humanities. It grew out of a seminar on contemporary multicultural writing in German at the University of Chicago. It is a volume translated by many hands from texts selected by me. Lilian M. Friedberg, a prize-winning translator and now a graduate student at the University of Illinois at Chicago, undertook a number of the translations but, most vitally for the project, made the texts uniform. Rather than translate into a gender-neutral idiom we have retained the generic masculine throughout in order to preserve the spirit of the German original, which does not employ the gender-inclusive options available in German. The volume is exemplary in its work method but also in its selection. The essays come primarily from Broder's book publications, as these reflect his sense of the most important of his journalistic contributions and the larger projects in which he has been engaged. We are grateful to him for reading the volume and giving us permission to translate his work for a larger, English-speaking audience.

## NOTES

1. Jan Tomasz Gross, *Sasiedzi: historia zaglady zydowskiego miasteczka* (Sejny: Pogranicze, 2000); translated by the author as *Neighbors: The Destruction of the Jewish Community in Jedwabne, Poland* (Princeton, N.J.: Princeton University Press, 2001). See Adam Michnick, "Poles and the Jews: How Deep the Guilt?" *New York Times,* 17 March 2001, and the answer by Leon Wieseltier, "Righteous," *New Republic,* 9 April 2001.

2. Qtd. in Angelika Königseder, *Flucht nach Berlin: Jüdische Displaced Persons, 1945–1948* (Berlin: Metropol, 1998), 36.

3. Qtd. in Susann Heenen-Wolff, *Im Haus des Henkers: Gespräche in Deutschland* (Frankfurt a. M.: Dvorah-Verlag, 1992), 267.

4. See Jeffrey Herf, *Divided Memory: The Nazi Past in the Two Germanys* (Cambridge, Mass.: Harvard University Press, 1997), 106–62.

5. Anson Rabinbach, "German Intellectuals and the Gulf War," *Dissent* (1991): 459–63.

A JEW IN THE NEW GERMANY

# WHY I WOULD RATHER NOT BE A JEW—
# AND IF I MUST, THEN RATHER NOT
# IN GERMANY

During the following year (1939) the Jews in Bonn, like those throughout the empire, had to give up their stores and factories. The solution that the Nationalist-Socialist regime offered for the problem of how the Jews should be expected to cover their living expenses once they had exhausted their savings was commonly known to be deportation to the death camps.

—From an article in the Municipal Information Service of the city of Bonn about Reichskristallnacht

It's the same with rats: you have to know where their nests are in order to exterminate them.

—Helmut Schirrmacher, president of the Law Enforcement Workers' Union, commenting in an interview with the *BILD-Zeitung* on how to combat terrorism

Many Jews lost their lives in the thirties and forties. Others had to move to foreign countries, where some of them came into good standing.

—*Die Odenwälder Heimatzeitung* in an article about Reichskristallnacht

When it came time for me to start school, my mother went to the director of
the Wilhelm Pieck School in Katowice, Poland, where we were living then, to
register me. My sister, nine years my senior, attended the same school. I still
remember well how my mother returned home completely distraught, explaining that the director had said there were already enough Jewish children en-
rolled in the school and that she had best find somewhere else to place me. My
father, then president of some craftsmen's association, went in there and raised
hell. That's how I got into the school that my mother wanted me to attend.

When I was a child we spent our summer vacations in a rented apartment in
Zoppot. One evening—I must have been eight or nine at the time—the doorbell
rang. Two men standing outside asked, "Are there any Jews living in this building?" Neither their tone of voice nor their posture left the impression that they
wanted to sit down and eat matzo with us. My mother said, "No, of course not!"
and quickly closed the door. Much later, she told me that this event had been
the last straw: this was what made my parents finally decide to leave Poland. In
April 1957 they left the People's Republic of Poland with their two children, my
sister and me. My sister, an enthusiastic Zionist at the time, went to Israel. She
has since relocated to Paris. My parents and I stayed in Vienna for a year; early
in 1958 we moved to Cologne. I went to the Gymnasium, completed my Abitur
eight years later, and became what one would call a freelance author.

I don't think it was easy for my parents to resettle on German soil. When
the war broke out, they left Katowice, which had belonged to Germany since
1918, and went to Krakow because they thought the Germans would reclaim
Katowice but never advance as far as Krakow. However, when the Nazis did
in fact occupy Krakow, my parents were sent to the ghetto, then from one concentration camp to another for three years. Most of my relatives were deported and murdered. My sister survived because she was hidden by a Catholic
family.

There were probably two reasons my parents decided to move to Germany in spite of everything: first, the unabated Polish anti-Semitism (there were still pogroms in Poland–even after the war–against Jews who had escaped the Nazis), and second, the opportunity to allow their children to live in the "free Western world" made possible by the so-called reparations–even though my parents were not outspoken anticommunists. Besides that, my father, like many eastern Jews, was a "German fanatic." He had already high-tailed it out of Galicia and headed for Berlin when I was still young enough to be sneaking into R-rated movies, my heart racing from the thrill of it and the fear of getting caught. Throughout his life, Berlin remained for him a symbol of grandeur, openness, and liberalism. In all seriousness, he maintained that the Berliners had not been Nazis. He cherished the Germans' dependability, diligence, precision, and pertinacity without realizing that these very virtues had been deployed in organizing the Final Solution to the Jewish Question.

Since my parents could prove they came from German culture and language circles, we had no difficulties obtaining citizenship. I can't even remember now the day we received German passports, though I do know exactly where I stashed the certificate verifying that we were no longer Polish citizens. Today, when I travel to the Netherlands or return from a trip to Denmark, it seems as though the officials checking my passport are a bit puzzled by it–but of course, that's probably just my imagination. At any rate, I have yet to become accustomed to traveling with a document that states right below my picture, "the bearer of this passport is a German." I am a citizen of the Federal Republic of Germany, but neither the official citizenship status nor the passport itself makes me a genuine German.

There are Jews, "passport Germans" like myself, who can pass for Germans but who resolve their identity crises by boasting of their Jewishness at every opportunity–however inappropriate it may be. To me, that is senseless babble from people who have nothing else to take pride in. You can only take pride in the things you can control. I have as much control over my Jewishness as I have over my eye color or shoe size. And, when I think about it, I would really rather not be a Jew.

Every time I travel through a picturesque countryside that looks as though it were tailor-made to suit the people living there, I wish I could be from there and live there now. I would have a farm, let's say in the northeastern province of Drente in the Netherlands. I would step outside my door every day at sunrise to assure myself that day still dawned without incident and that the world was just as the sun had left it the night before. I'd even be willing to accept the occasional flooding and the EU regulation of milk prices as part of the cost of living. Of course, it wouldn't have to be Drente, and it wouldn't have to be a farm. The point is that I just wish I could associate my heritage with something concrete, something I can relate to without getting sick at the thought of it.

Katowice, my birthplace, is located less than two hundred kilometers from Auschwitz. When I was born in 1946, the stench of Zyklon B still hung in the air. I must have taken in this smell along with my mother's milk. I can still smell it. Nothing was the subject of more discussion in our house than the time of persecution: how my mother survived an evacuation in a garbage can, how a young Jew who had no family voluntarily took my father's place when he was supposed to be deported, how my mother had to work in a quarry, how my father came down with typhus in a concentration camp, how a concentration camp's commander let prisoners be torn limb from limb by his dogs. These were horrible stories from an unimaginable world, a world where all your worst nightmares suddenly become reality.

It took a long time for me to understand that my parents, though they had just barely survived the physical experience of the camps, were psychologically devastated by it. Their emotional dissolution was "final," and they had to keep telling these stories again and again because otherwise, as time passed, they wouldn't believe they had in fact experienced and survived it. These stories must have left a strong impression on me, even though I didn't want to hear them, and despite the fact that I often left the room when my parents started telling them. Today I know those stories had a decisive impact on my development, and this is the Jewish part of my existence. It is something that is completely beyond my control, something that controls me the way *it* wants.

As I said, I am not proud of it; in fact, it is burdensome. I would happily give it up, if I could. And sometimes I think that if I didn't live in Germany, I might be able to give it up. But I sure as hell can't do that in Germany. When I am standing on a platform at the train station and hear an announcement that a train is arriving or departing "on schedule," the automatic association is the way the trains to the concentration camps were always right "on schedule." When I am watching TV and hear a news anchorman say, "Willi Peter Stoll, who was shot while fleeing arrest . . . ," then I know how the same man, in different times, would have formulated news updates about people who were shot "on the run."

I know that I surely jump to many unfair conclusions and that I think and talk like a "typical German" even when faced with situations I could experience anywhere (not only in Germany). For example, when I am at the supermarket and want to buy one cucumber. There is a sale: "three cucumbers for DM 1.15," and the check-out girl insists that I either take three or none. Or when I come to an empty parking lot and park my car in any old spot, then get scolded by the parking attendant because I didn't park in the spot he had assigned me. Of course, I know his whole purpose in life is to put people in their places. But I can't help thinking that, at the ramp to Auschwitz, he must have applied the same stupid obstinance and obsessive love of order to making sure that everyone got, and never left, his place in line.

That I could think such things does not come from being Jewish per se but rather from my *own* personal experience of being Jewish. I know many Jews who feel very comfortable living in Germany, who go about their business, demonstrate for the PLO, or even serve as press secretary for Franz Josef Strauß. Strauß, of course, marked a turning point in postwar history in 1969 with this sentence: "Any people that has demonstrated this level of economic achievement has a right not to have to hear any more about Auschwitz." And I know many non-Jews who are German both by birth and by ancestry who think and feel exactly as I do, who get upset about the same things. For the most part, I am better able to discuss these things with non-Jews than with Jews because for many Jews simply being able to walk around without a yellow star on their chest is enough to signal a normalization of life.

You can hardly fault people who survived Auschwitz for assuming such a stance, but I see no reason to adopt the same position for myself. It's not the "big problems" that make it clear to me what country I live in—the popularity of the neo-Nazi NPD or of *Die Nationalzeitung,* its official publication, or the percentage of former Nazis serving as high-ranking government officials. Rather, it is banal everyday news that has nothing to do with Jews, with German-Jewish relations—things that, at first glance, have nothing to do with Nazi mentality either. Let me illustrate what I mean with a few examples from the past couple of years:

- A housewife from Fulda was sentenced to a year and a half in prison without probation because she allegedly committed perjury. On the appeal, the sentence was reduced to one year with probation. Eleven witnesses confirmed her statement, while only one police officer disputed it. The court lent more credibility to the one police officer than to the eleven witnesses, each of whom it disqualified as a witness based on "mental incompetence."
- To accommodate the demonstrators expected to be arrested at an upcoming rally against the construction of a nuclear waste disposal plant in Gorleben, the government of the state of Lower Saxony transferred one hundred prisoners from the local jail into other already overcrowded facilities. The secretary of state at the Ministry of Justice in Lower Saxony explained to the press that, for him, it went without saying that the government should make preparations well in advance for arrests anticipated during upcoming demonstrations. Detainees should have "proper accommodations," because, as

he said, "We wouldn't want to leave the prisoners standing out in the rain, now would we?"

– In Hannover, a group of police broke down the door to a house during a search for terrorists. They threw tear gas through the skylights and ordered tenants to come out with their hands up. The tenants were detained for identification for twelve hours. After they had been identified, it was another twelve hours before they were released from police custody. When the press sought information, they were given the "runaround" for twenty-four hours. Officials from the police headquarters in Hannover sent reporters to the offices of the federal attorney, who sent them to the Ministry of the Interior in Hannover. From the ministry they were sent to the Federal Office of Criminal Investigations, and from there back to police headquarters.

Finally, the police commissioner confirmed that the two people who were taken into custody had cooperated in the identification process. When asked why it had taken twelve hours to release them, he simply refused to answer, stating instead that he was only responsible for questions that begin with "how" and not questions that begin with "why." Questions that begin with "why" were to be directed to the Office of the Federal Attorney.

– In a public speech, the minister of the interior (from Lower Saxony), Egbert Möcklinghoff (Christian Democratic Union), explained that Willy Brandt's appeal to "venture for increased democracy" was one of the "most dangerous phrases of the postwar period." For Möcklinghoff, democracy was in itself a "dangerous venture."

– In Heidelberg, there is a police policy for removing transient residents, forcing them to leave the city and settle in the outlying areas. Deploying language more appropriate to the deposition of hazardous waste, the program is called Verbringungsverwahrung, or "repository custody." A police spokesperson explained that giving the nonsedentary residents an "extended vacation" was a more appropriate way of achieving their goal than hauling them all off to the local precinct.

– A drill sergeant for the Panzer-Pioneer Division of the armed forces told new recruits that the most important tool of the Pioneer was "the combination pliers, which we need to rip out gold teeth from the dead Russians." He also told them that in order to preserve the valuable gold fillings, they should never shoot an enemy in the head, only in the torso.

– During the search for the Schleyer murderers, members of the security department were surprised by the public response.[1] The minister of the interior of Lower Saxony at the time, Groß, said: "The readiness to help the police has never been as evident as it is now." Word from the Ministry of the Interior in Nordrhein-Westfalen was that, "the public has taken this manhunt into its own hands." Police were most taken aback by the "readiness to cooperate" on the part of drivers–tens of thousands allowed their cars to be searched "without complaining and with a lot of tolerance."

- In Butzbach, a prison official jumped another customer in a bar and yelled, "You terrorist, you are going directly to jail!" He grabbed the man by the collar, dragged him outside, and stuffed him in the trunk of his own Mercedes. Then he drove to the prison, where he tried to unload his cargo. After the prison officials refused to accept it, he drove back to the center of town where he showed off his prisoner in another bar.
- After the burial in Stuttgart of Ensslin, Baader, and Raspe, key members of the RAF faction who committed suicide in prison, the names of the twelve hundred mourners were taken by the police. According to police statements, they were collected as "valuable evidence." In a letter to the *Frankfurter Rundschau*, three attorneys from Kassel reported additional tactics on the part of police: "A vehicle drove into the crowd repeatedly, unhindered by any intervention on the part of the police officers stationed nearby. The driver of the vehicle—as was later ascertained—was an officer in civilian dress. At the back of the procession, motorized police officers also drove into the crowd. These provocations continued until the people threatened by them responded in self-defense. That, of course, was the signal for the police officers to strike—demonstrators were thrown to the ground, battered, and kicked—with the enthusiastic support of catcalls from passersby."
- Seven hundred citizens of the city of Speyer were questioned by the Federal Office for the Protection of the Constitution of Rheinland-Pfälz. They had signed a petition to promote a teacher associated with the German Communist party. The Ministry of Culture, Education, and Church Affairs had handed the list over to the agency.
- In Duisberg, the police put an end to a private party after some neighbors complained about excessive noise, a disruption of the peace. Forty-two officers armed with machine guns and nightsticks drove the teenagers out of the house. They dragged the teenagers by the hair, hit them, threw them down stairs, and used tear gas.
- In Wahmbeck an der Weser, two police officers entered a house at six o'clock in the morning to forcibly bring a sixteen-year-old truant to vocational school. When the girl's sixty-two-year-old mother stood in their way and allegedly struck them with her lame husband's cane, the "keepers of order" used chemical weapons "in self-defense." Half an hour later, the woman was dead. The Office of the District Attorney in Göttingen halted the investigation against the two officers after establishing that the woman's death did not result from the deployment of tear gas but rather from the woman's heart condition, which was simply aggravated by the police call to her home. It is possible, admitted the district attorney's office, that the officers "might have become a bit harsh or out of line," but their conduct was "fundamentally legal" and remained within "the bounds or actions appropriate to the situation at hand." The Office of Public Affairs in charge of the

case had ordered the police to intervene after the girl had been absent from school for four days.

– In Regensburg, two students were sentenced to a fine of DM 450 each after they were charged with coercion and trespassing. They had organized a "happening" on school grounds with the intent of caricaturing the recruitment campaigns of the Bavarian Office for the Protection of the Constitution. Prepared with cardboard drawings, traditional Bavarian hats, and fake microphones, they interviewed fellow students who immediately proffered information about "terrorist" spokespeople and "left-wing" GEW teachers at the school.

The DA's office deemed this an "unauthorized assumption of authority." Moreover, they charged the two students with having brought the Office for the Protection of the Constitution "into disrepute" and forcibly shoving an educational director aside. A week after this verdict, information was released about a high school student in Bottrop who had spied on his teachers and schoolmates. The student happened to be president of the local student's union (which was closely affiliated with the CDU). The student had sold the written records to a man who had approached him as an agent of the government Office for the Protection of the Constitution.

– In conjunction with celebrations of the fortieth anniversary of the Reichskristallnacht, word got out that Hitler was still officially registered as an honorary citizen of the city of Hameln in Lower Saxony. The Social Democratic party faction demanded that this honorary citizenship be revoked. The administrative committee turned down the SPD faction's request because, according to the current bylaws, rights to honorary citizenship can only be withdrawn with the approval of the highest governing authority due to improper conduct of the honorary citizen. This was nevertheless an administrative act that could only take effect after notice had been served and would remain subject to appeal throughout the long drawn-out red-tape-plagued process. There was nothing more the committee could do at this time, since the person in question was deceased–with this explanation, the case was settled for both the city council and the majority in the SPD faction.

✳

This selection is of course arbitrary but not atypical. It's not about (social) faux pas but rather about practical evidence of a consciousness that should not be considered "fascist" or "Nazi," because these adjectives skirt around the issue. They restrict it and enshroud it in an air of *haut gaut,* thus enabling everyone to easily distance himself from the terms. These are incidents that may occur anywhere in the world, but nowhere with the same frequency and in such unadulterated form as in the "pure culture" of Germany: this is that utterly proper German formalism rearing its head here, the same thing that quite properly initiated genocide with the decree of the Nuremberg Laws. It is the desire on the part of the German citizen who was never a *citoyen* to subject himself to self-prescribed subjugation, denunciation, and the gatekeeper's game. It is the misanthropic audacity of the German bureaucrat who will stop at nothing–even if it entails going over someone else's dead body–as long as he can justify it based on some term of his employment contract. It is the unrelenting German notion that the state can take away any right and that citizens owe the state loyalty and gratitude, not that the state is a public service enterprise for its citizens to avail themselves of at will. It is the German compulsion to sanitize, eliminate, and eradicate. It is the endeavor to restrict social consensus about what is and isn't permissible to a bare minimum and to ostracize deviants for disrupting the pursuant harmony. It is the German arrogance that can't even be curtailed in the interest of strategic considerations: the German TV station ZDF demanded that The Hague release a list of the names of 140 Dutch reporters who had lambasted Helmut Kohl with their audacious questions. Or the way the Landestags-President in Lower Saxony announced that the CDU planned on going from town to town with a copy of this broadcast to demonstrate the way Kohl had interceded on behalf of the Fatherland in The Hague. Or perhaps the letter to the editor that stated: "Like every smaller nation of people living next to a bigger neighbor, the Dutch have an inferiority complex. . . ."

I can't listen anymore to the prattle about the "other Germany," assumed to have risen from the ruins of the Nazi regime on the night of May 8–9, 1945. The "other Germany" can't afford to name the University of Oldenburg after the Nobel Prize–winning (1936) dissident journalist who was incarcerated by the Nazis, Karl von Ossietzky, or the University in Düsseldorf after Heinrich Heine; it can, however, afford the Agnes Miegel and Hermann Burte Schools, named after the writer Agnes Miegel, known as the "mother of East Prussia," and the devout National-Socialist opera writer Hermann Burte, respectively. The "other Germany" saw no need to compensate the gypsies, homosexuals, and communists who had been in concentration camps.

The "other Germany" deems it appropriate and consistent with constitutional law to dispute the pension plans of Republican Militia veterans who fought in the Spanish Civil War yet never fails to disburse payment to former members of the fascist legion Condor. The "other Germany" put up with the incumbent president who refused to overturn the court decision in the case of a sixteen-year-old boy executed by the Nazis in 1944. The president justified his veto by citing testimony given by the very Gestapo members who'd sent the boy to his death in the first place.

There is no such thing as the other Germany! It's still the same old Germany that has always been, a German character with a will to cure the whole world of its ills—or, as the popular late nineteenth- and early twentieth-century saying went, *Am deutschen Wesen soll die Welt genesen!* that is, "The German nation shall be the world's salvation!" This German national character, or "deutsches Wesen," once it was denied the opportunity for expansion beyond its borders, intensified the process of inner colonization at home—of course, that doesn't mean it abandoned the inner colonization once it was again able to go to work beyond its borders. It's still the same Germany that devoutly enacts its "persecuted innocence" (Karl Kraus) and continues to pursue this tradition under the auspices of an ostensibly democratic system foisted upon it by way of ordinance.

There is no other Germany, there are only other Germans. But there have always been other Germans: many people who suffer miserable conditions, work their fingers to the bone—and never get ahead. And I know that those other Germans are worth their weight in gold to the real Germany—oh, what pains are taken on their behalf and how they are showered with commemoration.

Just recently, I met a German emigre living in Amsterdam who voluntarily left Germany in 1937. He is not a Jew; he was not a communist; he wasn't even particularly political. Moreover, he had a good position at a radio station that he could have kept with only minimal conformity on his part. He left Germany because he did not want to live in a country controlled by the National Socialists. During the German occupation of the Netherlands he hid ten people in his two-bedroom apartment. He saved their lives. He has a good reputation in the Netherlands and was honored by the Yad Vashem Institute in Israel. But it has yet to occur to anyone in the "other Germany" to check in on him or even to bother to ask whether he can get by on his meager income—not a soul! There were and are many such people that the "other Germany" must be proud of, but since no official channel has been established for their acknowledgment or registration, no one feels responsible for them. And yet sending retirement funds to former Nazis living in South American exile seems to function flawlessly.

As *a Jew* I don't have to get upset about all this, as *a Jew* it does not concern me; no one has anything against me. When *Die Welt* and its philo-Semitic Messrs. Springer and Co. want to badmouth me, they write: "Henric M. Broder, an author operating from an extreme left-wing position, writing for all the usual extreme left-wing rags. . . ." When a writer for the *Rheinische Merkur* wants to denounce me, he writes: "Henryk M. Broder, a left-leaning WDR-author, even better known as a star columnist for glossy girly mags situated on the extreme left. . . ."

I always hesitate for a moment, and even though my fingers itch to respond, I ask my friends Friedhelm, Hanno, and Uwe what I should do, then let it go because they say "don't do it." Besides, what would I say? How would I respond to this drill-sergeant mentality ("operating author"), to this puritanical beating around the bush ("girly mags")? Perhaps by pointing out that *Playboy* also ranks among the rags "situated on the extreme left," or that I have written countless stories about corrupt left-wingers? Am I supposed to define myself as being anything but left-wing in comparison to *Die Welt* and the *Rheinische Merkur?* No respectable non-Jew would bother to respond by refuting the charge of being a left-winger. So I don't react and instead take note of just how little it takes to be branded as a left-winger in this country of destroyers and deniers—one clever word and you're branded as a communist. Oddly enough, the Federal Republic is likely the only democratic country in which the label "left-wing" is considered defamatory—utterly unthinkable in France, Italy, Holland, England, or even in America.

*Die Welt* considered it objectionable that "Henryk M. Broder, of all people," was allowed to broadcast a special about extreme right-wing publishers on the West German public radio station (WDR). In their day, the Nazi newspapers *Stürmer* and *Völkische Beobachter* considered it objectionable that Jews, of all people, would offer resistance against anti-Semitism. I know that those people who attack me today as a "left-winger" would also like to attack me as "a Jew" if it came to *that*, because we are dealing here with the same character types with the same instincts; they have only shifted the focus of their negativity to different targets. First and foremost, I have to contend with the absurdity of the fact that for me it's not the anti-Semites who pose the problem but rather self-proclaimed "friends of Jews," on the one hand, and "career Jews," on the other.

During the twenty-two years that I have lived in the Federal Republic, I have only been the object of an openly anti-Semitic attack twice. The first time was shortly after my arrival, and it set the stage for my life here. I had only been in school a few days (a horrible math and science academy) when a classmate came up to me. He was my age—about eleven. He looked me straight in the eye and said, very calmly: "They forgot to gas you." Presumably, he had checked the class roster and found, in the column labeled "religious denomination," the entry "Mosaic" beside my name. And when he asked at home what it meant, he was instructed accordingly.

The second attack, twenty years later, was staged at a very different level. In a weekly newspaper known less for its journalistic quality than for being a megaphone for the party line, I was introduced with these words: "der in Deutschland lebende Journalist Henryk M. Boder"—that is, "Henryk Broder, a journalist residing in Germany." This was a subtle, but clear reference to my "foreign" origin, my not belonging to the "authentic" German Volksganzen. This sentence did not appear in the Nazi publication, *Die Deutsche National-Zeitung,* but rather on January 6, 1978, in the German Jewish weekly, *Die Allgemeine Wochenzeitung.* It wasn't written by some neo-Nazi hack but by Heinz Galinski, the coeditor of the *Allgemein* and, for as long as anyone can remember, chairman of the Jewish Council in West Berlin.

In a longer article entitled "Verleumdungen deines trojanischen Esels"–or, loosely translated, "Slanderous Greetings from Your Friend, the Trojan Ass"–Galinski tore me to shreds. The article was about a speech on neo-Nazi intrigues that I had delivered at the Jewish Council in Zurich. In it I made a few critical statements about Jewish-German relations and commented on the arrogant airs of a few Jewish representatives. Heinz Galinski did not actually attend the lecture. His indignation was based on an article published in the *Baseler Jüdischen Rundschau* about my talk. Galinski was as incensed by a positive review of the lecture in the *Jüdischen Rundschau* as he was by the lecture itself. But the only thing he quoted verbatim from the lecture was my concluding statement: "The Germans got the Jews they deserve." Galinski could only see this "as a sick defamation of the Jewish community in Germany." "Even words like defamation and denigration are not too strong to characterize what Broder said about us." In point of fact, Galinski had no idea what I actually said "about us" because he was familiar with my lecture only from the review. His venom was inspired by a few citations taken out of context, like the concluding statement mentioned above.

But what little he could glean from that was sufficient to prompt West Berlin's Number One Jew to make far-reaching speculations about my motives: "Perhaps, our spiritual incorruptibility bothers him. [Broder] is openly troubled by the fact that we . . . never let our eye for proportions dim, that we are as little blind in the left eye as we are in the right, that we have protected the Federal Republic of Germany from the distorted representations prevailing under the current circumstances . . . from powers that have nothing in common with the issues and concerns of the Jewish community, with the goal of weakening parliamentary democracy in all of Europe and to make its supporters question it." In one fell swoop, Galinski, brandishing his own peculiar grandiosity, managed to relegate me to the realm of obscurity and pat himself on his own pro-democratic back. The only thing lacking in his criticism was the observation that the Jewish-Bolshevik Broder was a threat to the entire Christian West.

I wrote a reply to Galinski and sent it to the *Allgemein,* assuming they would be fair enough to allow the target of his attack the opportunity to respond. My statement was never printed. It wasn't even sent back. A few weeks later, it was published in *Extra Dienst,* a small newspaper circulated only in Berlin, which, of course, does not have the same readership as the *Allgemein,* but anyway. . . .

In the direct aftermath of my trip to Zurich, I had the privilege of experiencing the degree of sensibility the official representatives of Jews residing in Germany are able to muster in their reactions to certain situations—ever contingent on whether or not they are directly affected by them. Customs officials at the Cologne/Bonn airport had tried to photocopy my lecture notes before my departure. I reported the incident in the *Frankfurter Rundschau,* and parliamentary inquiries about the incident ensued. A couple of journalists and Members of Parliament pursued the matter, and gradually the various legally borderline methods the Federal Border Police had employed were made public. Ultimately, Minister of the Interior Maihofer, who had been under fire since the Bugging Scandal, was forced to resign.[2]

Immediately following the incident at the airport, I wrote a letter to Werner Nachmann, the president of the Board of Directors of the Central Jewish Council in Germany, asking him whether the Federal Border Police's interest in a manuscript on Nazi intrigues might not merit the Jewish Council's attention to the matter. That was on December 21, 1977. More than two months later, on February 28, 1978, I lodged another formal complaint in a second letter to Nachmann: "To date, I have yet to receive a reply, nor so much as an acknowledgement of receipt. I would request that you please be kind enough to inform me as to whether you have received my correspondence and whether or not you intend to take action in this matter." In a reply dated March 10, 1978, the president of the Board of Directors answered: "I am in receipt of both your letter of December 21 and that of February 28. From the information you supplied, I gathered that you had registered your complaint about this incident directly to the Ministry of the Interior and I have taken note of this." That was it. Surely, I thought, this can't be the end of it.

On March 23, 1978, I wrote a third letter to Werner Nachmann: "After it took you almost three months to formulate a five-line response, I would again request that you clarify whether or not you, or rather, the Central Office, intend to take any action in the incident involving customs officials' inspection of a manuscript for a lecture on Nazi intrigues in the Federal Republic. In the event that you do not intend to act, I would greatly appreciate receiving official confirmation of the fact that this incident is of no concern to the Central Jewish Council. Perhaps you will find time to write me between army reserve exercises. I would appreciate not having to wait another three months for an answer."

This time Werner Nachmann answered almost immediately. In a letter dated March 30, 1978, he wrote: "Based on the tone of your letter dated March 23, I have to ask you to please correspond directly with the Secretary General of the Central Office from now on and not with me."

Werner Nachmann evidently considered it in bad form for *me* to mention *his* career as an army reserve officer. But, only a few weeks after our brief exchange, he would demonstrate in which cases and exactly how he was prepared to intervene, without regard to protocol. In May 1978, Nachmann assured then minister president of Baden-Wurttemberg, the former NS naval judge Hans Karl Filbinger, that, in spite of Rolf Hochhuth's description of him as a "lousy pedantic lawyer," Filbinger was a fine upstanding person who had made substantial contributions to rebuilding Jewish communities. Headlines in *Die Welt* exalted: "Jewish Spokesman Commends Filbinger's Political Efforts." As a matter of fact, the Germans *have* gotten the Jews that they need and deserve.

Perhaps no one is better equipped to illustrate the degree of tastelessness a Jew is capable of when it comes to demonstrating servility to his non-Jewish environment than Berlin's quiz- and talk-show host Hans Rosenthal, even when it's not expected of him. He just couldn't resist officiating ZDF's game show "Dalli-Dalli" on November 9, the anniversary of Reichskristallnacht. In response to a petition spearheaded by a Jewish teenager, and which I had also signed, Rosenthal informed me in writing that he felt he had been unfairly attacked. "Months ago, I personally requested that the Dalli-Dalli slot be switched from the ninth of November to another night. Aside from the fact that I made mention of the date's significance when the show aired on November 9 and actually changed the program's content accordingly, no one seems to understand that a moderator who is not even on the payroll but rather an independent contractor is not in a position to influence program scheduling. The best he can do is submit a request."

But what would have happened if Hans Rosenthal hadn't merely *asked* for a rescheduling? What if he had calmly, but resolutely, said: "No, not on November 9"? Nothing would have happened except that he would have gained a degree of respect among any number of fine, upstanding people whom he is not likely to win over in the next twenty years with his broadcasts. Of course, an "independent contractor" cannot reschedule programming, but he *can* certainly say that he will not, under any circumstances, schedule anything on a particular date. This is especially so when the "independent contractor" is head of the department at Radio in the American Sector (RIAS), a partner in West Berlin's Spielbank Casino, and has diverse other sources of income that situate him such that he is economically independent enough not to have to rely on his income as an "independent contractor." It is quite simply a moral question: whether commemorating the victims of pogroms takes precedence over forcing the editorial staff in ZDF's entertainment department to reconfigure its schedule.

On November 30, 1978, the representative assembly of the Jewish Council of Berlin, the council parliament, issued a written defense of its chairman, Hans Rosenthal. The assembly saw no reason to find fault with Rosenthal's conduct, since he had attempted, as early as October 1977, "to have the airing of the broadcast changed to another day." The Board of Directors of the Central Office had been informed about the scheduled broadcast but "did not take any steps to get the program switched to another time slot." But Hans Rosenthal "*had* informed" the president of the Central Council "of the scheduled broadcast." The ultimate conclusion of the exculpatory brief: "Since the decisive question involved his ability to practice or not to practice his profession, Hans Rosenthal had no choice but to go through with the broadcast." This then, was the uniquely Jewish rendering of what it means to operate under direct orders in a state of exception–a matter of the ability to practice or not to practice one's profession, a dilemma from which Hans Rosenthal could not extricate himself. Since the board did not take on the matter, neither did Hans Rosenthal.

It is worth taking another look at the text of this explanation: "he *had* informed," "steps taken," "the decisive question involved," "go through with the broadcast"; these are the words that flow so effortlessly from the lips of council representatives comfortably situated high above the rest of us. These representatives are oblivious to the fact that their word selection alone adopts the same ideology of justification employed by millions of Germans long before them in order to talk themselves out of any sense of personal culpability in having looked the other way, having heard nothing, and simply having gone along with the program. At least as far as hypocrisy is concerned, the German-Jewish symbiosis is in full force.

Much has already been said and written about the official representatives of the Jews living in Germany. There is a "Central Office." The office has a "Board of Directors," the board has a president, and that is Herr Werner Nachmann in Karlsruhe. In addition, the Central Office has a "Secretary" whose seat is located in the "Secretary General's" office, and that secretary is Alexander Ginsburg in Düsseldorf. A special role is played by the director of the biggest Jewish Council, who happens to be Heinz Galinski in West Berlin. The singularity of his role derives from the fact that Mr. Galinski considers himself the real spokesman for the Jewish community and considers Messrs. Ginsburg and Nachmann completely incompetent–and of course, the feeling is mutual. The question, for example, of who should write the feature story on the front page of the *Allgemein* (edited by Heinz Galinski and Alexander Ginsburg, or vice-versa), and whose name should be printed in what size font, comprises a large part of their personal platforms for program debates.

This is a Jewish joke without the humor, a dwarf opera in CinemaScope®. These men are so caught up in their internal conflicts and their desire to foster contacts with German patrons that they don't even realize or, wherever possible, overlook the fact that for years German agencies have again been promoting a "Jewish policy" with the same diligence that culminated in the consummation of the Nuremberg Laws. Until the mid-1960s, Jewish refugees and displaced persons from Eastern Europe were taken in with open arms. Today a Jewish Spätaussiedler–an East European emigrant of German origin– hardly has a chance at being considered a homeland exile. Moreover, the authorities in charge dwell painstakingly on the study of old files and through this study–no pain, no gain–arrive at completely different conclusions.

In a letter dated February 2, 1979, the senior commissioner of the city of Mönchengladbach communicated to the Jew Max B. the October 25, 1961, "decision of the former district of Grevenbroich" (whose judicial successor is the city of Mönchengladbach) confirming that Max B.'s status as an exile was being reversed and his A-status Exile ID card revoked. So, after Max B. had been recognized as an exile for *eighteen* years, the exile officer deemed it necessary to reexamine the case and to rule on it again. The expressed reason for this decision was that "an examination of procedure protocols from 1961" revealed "that neither your mother nor your foster parents had issued a statement of commitment to German national character pursuant to Statute 6 of the BVFG³ and that you are thus not entitled to be categorized as a German national." At the first ruling in 1961, "the facts of the case had been incorrectly categorized under the legal prerequisites determining claims."

The case of Max B. is no exception; there are hundreds, possibly even thousands of similar cases. In a "statement about the treatment of Jewish emigrants and refugees in Germany" issued in July 1977, the "association of Jewish Displaced Persons" reports an "investigative hysteria" that recalls "fatal associations to the years between 1933 and 1945."

As soon as one realizes that there is no explicit mandate from the federal government or the state governments to discriminate against Jewish applicants, then the measures and pronouncements of the representative offices must be traced back to the initiatives and peculiarities of the particular officials within them. In a decision made by the Refugee Office of the city of Offenbach in November 1976, there is the horrific sentence about the conditions in the concentration camp in Plaszow: "very often, camp inmates were shot to death with or without reason."

The Official Homeland Information Offices, or Heimatauskunftsstellen, agencies that supply the courts with data about the "Germanness" of specific applicants, operate on the assumption that Jews cannot be Germans. A typical justification for this stance is as follows: since a Jew of Romanian descent "did not participate" in the German resettlement implemented in 1940(!), he cannot be regarded as a German national. Or, based on the fact that an applicant lives on a predominantly Jewish street, the conclusion is drawn that the applicant acknowledges his allegiance to the Jewish people and therefore cannot be a German national. In a legal opinion issued by one Homeland Information Office, the credibility of an Aryan witness's testimony was once called into question because he was married to a Jew. In the course of the investigations conducted against people who had allegedly obtained certification of their status under false pretenses, elderly refugees were treated like felons and processed by the Criminal Identification Department, that is, fingerprints and mug shots were taken.

In at least once case, the investigator's inquiries led to the applicant's death: One day in April 1976, several criminal investigators forcibly entered the home of a Jew in Frankfurt and explained that they were looking for "evidence" without bothering to say for what evidence and for what purpose. The terminally ill sixty-eight-year-old man suffered a heart attack and died in the presence of his "guests." The obituary in the newsletter of the Jewish homeland-exiles stated, "we are all deeply shocked by the tragic circumstances surround his unexpected death." Five months after the unexpected death, his widow received a letter from the public prosecutor's office, establishing which alleged crime had caused the "tragic circumstances": "I herewith confirm that the investigations conducted against your deceased husband did not reveal sufficient evidence to merit criminal proceedings against him in conjunction with his submission of an application for displaced person status for yourself or your deceased husband."

It is not entirely unheard of that a public prosecutor has told a Homeland Information Office exactly what information he would like to receive. A public prosecutor from Ludwigshafen did just that in his letter to the second Homeland Information Office in Poland in November 1975. He requested evidence that "proves with certainty that the accused can not be considered a German pursuant to paragraph 6 of the BVFG."

German officials are not swayed by ethics or moral obligations in their decisions. When it comes to their choice of methods, procuring expert opinions or subpoenaing witnesses, neither humanitarian scruples nor jurisdictional considerations serve to keep German investigators in check. This is demonstrated by their choice of methods, their manner of gathering evidence, and their selection of witnesses. For them, the end justifies the means—and that end is to prevent too many Jews from being recognized as German nationals. They will do anything to meet that end. To verify whether the applicants, a Jewish couple, Mr. and Mrs. Y. from Riga, were acknowledged as German people before the war, the government of Lower Franconia questioned an Aryan Displaced Person from Riga.

In a letter dated January 17, 1978, the Aryan wrote the government of Lower Franconia: "After 1934 the German population in the Balkans was registered and organized of their own volition into 'neighborhoods,' which were overseen by volunteers from the community. For example, my wife was overseer for the German families of Gertrude Street 56–73 with the title 'Nachbarschaftsführerin.' At the same time, I acted as 'block leader' and was in charge of six neighborhoods under the charge of a district leader for the German-Baltic Volksgemeinshaft. The job was done on a volunteer basis and completed based on a common commitment to nationalist ideals.

"Salomon Y. and his wife were not registered in the 'neighborhood' because they did not subscribe to the ideals on which the community was founded. . . . Jews, as well as half-Jews, Latvians, and Russians, were not allowed to join German organizations. It was considered a 'social offense' for German Balkans to associate with Jews. In the business and economic sectors, we would not be able to manage without the Jews, but the line was clearly understood throughout the community. Any woman or man who consented to a mixed marriage was automatically expelled from the German-Baltic society. The strict adherence to a consciousness of the German Volkstum abroad is based on the healthy maintenance of the national body in opposition to the other nationality groups and has not 'Nazi' tendencies. I would advise you to ask Mr. and Mrs. Salomon Y. the following trick questions: (1) Why did he name his son a typical Jewish name like 'Josef' even though the tendency at the time was to use German first names? (2) Is Y. still a member of the Hebrew or Mosaic faith? He could have converted to the Christian faith, because that was a common practice in Latvia after 1935/36. . . ."

Mr. and Mrs. Y. were denied recognition as German people and displaced persons based on *this* "affadavit." Perhaps the Jews, who behave like idiots just for the sake of being acknowledged as Germans, deserve no better treatment. They have earned nothing better because they still haven't had enough of the German master race, because they obviously haven't had enough torture and degradation. Still, the question is why different, stricter rules are applicable for determining whether or not Jews are "loyal to the German people" than those used to determine the same with regard to the Spätaussiedler from Poland or the Soviet Union who don't Germanize their names or learn German until after they've arrived in the Federal Republic, yet whose affiliation with German linguistic and cultural circles is never doubted.

The determining factor is whether one is a "Jew or non-Jew." When the notion that a Jew can't be German is promulgated in official German rhetoric and practice, then this may in fact be true. But this should have been clarified long ago, in 1945 at the latest, as soon as the Nuremberg Laws—which were unambiguous in this regard—were no longer in effect. Back then, of course, every Jew who returned to resettle on German soil was a welcome token figure. Jews in Germany—why, that was living proof of the fact that life had returned to normal and demonstrated to the entire world the transformation the Zeitgeist had undergone. This was, just like the so-called reparations, Germany's price of admission to the international "family of man." It was Germany's way of completely dissociating itself from the Nazi Germans.

Meanwhile—now that the postwar period is over and "we" are recognized by the world again—the Federal Republic has deemed such goodwill gestures superfluous. But with thirty thousand Jews living among sixty million Aryans—that is, 0.05 percent of the population—the Jewish population has again reached the degree of demographic density needed to justify the reimplementation of political policies for handling Jews. The matter is being played out in the public eye, but no one seems bothered by it. Has anyone even heard about it? Has an hour of silence commemorating the "Week of Brotherhood" been cancelled because of it? Has anyone from the Central Office of the Jews in Germany—ostensible representatives of Jewish social interests in Germany—slammed his fists on the table and yelled, "This is not the way it is going to be"? Has any one of the babbling idiots promoting common celebration of Christian-Jewish holidays suggested storming the offices of the authorities instead of pontificating "tolerance"?

What is happening in this country so rapidly coming into its own is bad. That this can all happen unhindered, that no one stays the hands of the bureaucrats who would still organize pogroms and evacuations if they were ordered to is spooky and makes clear that nothing has changed: neither in the political climate nor in the consciousness of the people who control it.

What was law then cannot be outlawed now.

—Hans-Karl Filbinger

Two Jews in a concentration camp. One says to the other: "Moishe, go ask the SS man over there what they have in store for us." Moishe: "Stop it, Shlomo. Just stop provoking. The Germans can be beastly."

Of course, we will do all we can now and in the future to strengthen the reputation of the German democracy abroad. . . . I see that my job is to always represent the right image of Germany, its citizens and parties, when there is a tendency to conjure up the specter of the "evil German."

> —Werner Nachmann, chairman of the Board of Directors of the Central Office of Jews in Germany

*Translated by Karen Walton*

## TRANSLATOR'S NOTES

1. Hanns-Martin Schleyer, a former Nazi and for many years later a high-ranking German captain of industry, was kidnapped and killed by the Red Army Faction in 1977 when he was president of the German Employers' Association.

2. Commonly known in Germany as the "Wanzen-Affäre," Broder refers here to the 1976–77 scandal in which Werner Maihofer, then minister of the interior, had been responsible for violations of constitutional law by ordering that recording devices be planted in the home of the nuclear physicist Klaus Traube in order to monitor his activities.

3. Bundesvertriebenen- und Flüchtlingsgesetz. Refers to provisions introduced in 1953 to the Federal Constitution (Basic Law) that regulate the repatriation of "expellees and refugees" as German nationals.

# YOU ARE STILL

# YOUR PARENTS' CHILDREN

## THE NEW GERMAN LEFT AND EVERYDAY ANTI-SEMITISM

My more or less dear left-wing friends![1]

I'm writing this letter because I no longer have any desire to talk to you. I just want to get a few things off my chest and on the record. It won't make anything better, but it will make some things clearer. And that is my sole concern.

A couple of weeks ago, I was in a so-called countercultural pub. On the walls—posters about Chile, El Salvador, Iran; on the tables—an appeal for solidarity with the imprisoned IRA comrades; in the bathroom—sayings carved in the wall, among others: "We are the people your parents warned you about!" Great, I thought, they are proud of their parents' mistakes!

You think you are so much different from your parents. You have, so it seems, achieved something no generation before you has ever accomplished: you have severed yourself completely from the tree from which you fell. A few days ago, I read an interview with some progressive punk-rocker types in the *taz*, Berlin's left-wing daily newspaper. In answer to the question, "What do you guys think about fascism?" one of these twentysomethings replied: "I didn't stick no Jew in the KZ; I didn't shoot no Poles; I really don't got nothing to do with that, that was my father or my grandfather. I don't blame my grandmother or my ancestors for the Thirty Years' War, neither. . . ." Another one of the punk rockers was quick to bridge past and present by saying: "Back then they gassed the Jews; today people are executed in Stammheim."[2]

Not everything that falls from the lips of "counterc”culturals" sounds so trite and stupid. But these statements set precisely those parameters that constrict the growth of your own historical consciousness: You "really have nothing to do" with your history. So the thought of what your parents did to the Jews comes to mind, if at all, only when you complain about how badly some social groups are being treated today. Women, students, or gays become the "Jews of today"; you are as oblivious to the audacity of such comparisons as you are to the fact that, in constructing them, you place yourselves in the immediate proximity of right-wing politicians like Strauß, Stoiber, and Kohl, who consider it appropriate to equate the anti-Strauß campaign with the Jew-baiting of *Der Stürmer*. You, too, abuse millions of dead for your everyday political agendas. You have lost all your principles, if you ever had any.

I could give you credit for some mitigating circumstances: your parents have abandoned you. What little you do know about your own history you have picked up by chance. You can distance yourselves from mom and dad as far as you wish, and speak as disparagingly of your procreators as you will—but you are still your parents' children. It is only in your conscious behavior, the part you can control, that you have set yourselves apart from your parents—the more pronounced the differentiation, the more contrived.

The reason for my complaint is that you refuse to recognize the coherence of cause and effect when it comes to yourselves, and you act as though you were a new breed of people: unburdened by the smell of the kitchens from which you come, born into a vacuum that didn't begin to fill until you appeared. That you absorbed more in your cradle than just the sound of a baby's rattle, that you have been fed not only on milk porridge but also on your mothers' and fathers' prejudice and predilection, on their way of thinking and feeling—this is a thought you haven't let concern you to this day.

The "pathologically clear conscience" of your parents—people who knew nothing and, if anything, only went along with it to prevent worse from happening: that pathologically clear conscience is your political seed money. With Auschwitz at your backs, but neither in your heads nor hearts, today you can afford to debate about whether refugees fleeing Vietnam are "real" or simply "economic refugees" who don't want to participate in the construction of socialism, and you count the dollar notes and gold bars these people bring along–those fortunate enough to survive their "flight." These debates took place here once before, when what was at stake was whether to let the wealthy Jews emigrate "for a fee" or whether to kill them right off the bat.

You have inherited your parents' racism and molded it to suit your own purposes. It's not the "what" that has changed but the "way": the way you concern yourselves with the Third World, the way you differentiate the good liberation movements from the bad according to the extent to which each satisfies your own revolutionary demands. Your willingness to conceal atrocities or even support them with propaganda as long as they are committed by your ideological allies against the right enemies exposes you as the talented offspring of those who quelled the Boxer uprising in China and liquidated the Hereros in South Africa. Of course, you don't dirty your *own* hands anymore–instead, you work seated at a "countercultural" desk or standing behind the counter of a revolutionary bar.

I want to elaborate here only on that part of your racist reservoir that concerns me in particular: your anti-Semitism. That a left-winger cannot, by nature, so to speak, be an anti-Semite because this is the domain of the right wing is as popular an excuse as it is deceptive. And you cling to it. The blanket absolution you confer upon yourselves is further evidence of your lack of historical awareness. I bet the names Slansky and Rajk don't even ring a bell, and the Physicians' Trial in 1953 sounds to you like a series on the conflict between Hackethal and classical medicine.[3]

Why can't a left-winger be an anti-Semite? Are left-wingers better people per se? Don't left-wingers beat their wives and discriminate against gays? Your racism begins with the overestimation of your own morality. Granted, you don't scrawl swastikas on the walls and can readily distance yourselves from that epithet "Judah, to hell with you!" You aren't that primitive–but the editors of the magazine *Das Reich* were just as embarrassed by the pejorative abuses printed in *Der Stürmer*.[4] Your anti-Semitism is subtle, refined by your consciousness and adapted to your political environment. I'll explain what I mean with a few concrete examples.

Late in 1978 West Berlin's Gallery 70 organized an exhibition on the subject of neo-Nazism. During the course of the exhibit's several-week run, discussions took place regularly at the gallery. I attended one–at issue were neo-Nazi incidents in West Berlin's schools. Around 150 teachers, most of them members of the German Educators' Union (GEW), reported on their experiences with extreme right-wing pupils in the attempt to assess fascist potential among youth. During the discussion, a young teacher–she was perhaps thirty years old–made the following statements: "Young people try to defend themselves against the dissemination of false information. The fact is that the concentration camps were first and foremost work camps, where artillery was produced cheaply, and only towards the end of the war, when defeat was foreseeable, did the Nazis begin the annihilation of the Jews. Today the Holocaust is used as Zionistic propaganda to justify the existence of the State of Israel." I was speechless. It sounded as though she'd recited these lines straight from the *Nationalzeitung*. I looked at the teacher, a young lady with henna red hair, decently dressed in countercultural attire, and thought: "She must be about to follow up on that statement, she could not have meant what she just said. . . ." But she had said exactly what she meant. And the best thing about it was: nobody refuted her! Not one of the roughly 150 teachers stood up and said: "Look lady, either you're talking total nonsense or you're trying to test us, but we aren't about to fall into that kind of trap. . . ." Nothing happened. There were further discussions about extreme right-wing and fascist viewpoints among the pupils. I left the gallery convinced from head to toe: if these are the guarantors of an antifascist education, then the Viking youth don't need to do anything on their own initiative—these crammers are their best accomplices.

In the summer of 1980 I attended a discussion at a Literatrubel, a literary coffee klatsch in Hamburg. One young man took the floor and, addressing a not particularly significant statement I'd made, said that he agreed with me completely and was familiar with my work, but he had one problem: as an ally in the antifascist struggle, he had tremendous respect for me, but he couldn't accept my Zionism. He was completely at odds with my position on the State of Israel. I said nothing. I didn't have the slightest desire to so much as ask this guy what a Jew would have to do to be accepted today. This antifascist was doing the same thing his parents had done: he determined what he would like a Jew to do in order to deal with him or utilize him for his own purposes. At that moment, I decided to leave the antifascist struggle to those who needed it most.

I have, as you perhaps know, worked for a long time on a subject that might better appeal to you: neo-Nazism. For over two years I haven't said or written another word about it because I realized that this debate conceals more than it reveals. Everyone in this country—Franz Josef Strauß and yourselves included—can, with a clear conscience, disassociate themselves from swastika scrawlers and Adolf Hitler fans who still celebrate April 20. Outrage over such antiquated expressions of Nazi sentiments clears the air and at the same time obscures from view the fascist "alter ego" in Mr. and Mrs. Everyman—and that includes you. A swastika on a house wall, an SS rune at a bus stop, a "Jews out!" on a Jewish shop—these are all anachronisms: forms of resentment shrouded in an aura of what borders on nostalgia. You, on the contrary, are right in step with the times. Gerhard Zwerenz, for example, makes a Jewish real estate broker and landowner his protagonist precisely because, as is common knowledge, there are so few Aryan representatives of this "breed" in this country.[5] The fact that it was directed against Jewish speculators played a decisive role in the squatters' movements in Frankfurt. We've been through all this before: as long as the major department stores were still under Jewish ownership, slogans circulated about the "Department Store Plague." Pamphlets calling for people to gather at "mass rallies" read: "The Jew came and set up department stores right under the German merchant's nose; he destroyed his existence with his flamboyant, hard-sell advertising; he took the craftsmen's bread away; he put a stranglehold on the traders' neck. . . ." Later, after the department stores had been Aryanized, no one got worked up over the fact that they threatened the existence of small businesses as much as they had under Jewish owners. We're lucky the Jews haven't been credited with the decline of Berlin's Kreuzberg district–it's hard to imagine how this would fuel your imagination.

Your parents may have abided by the motto, "The Jews are our misfortune!" (or, "The Jews are to blame for everything!"), but, in the absence of Jewish multitudes, you have had to adapt the principle slightly. You just say: "Things Jewish are to blame!"

In October 1979 I published an essay in *Konkret* titled "I Am a Chauvinist" in which I declare my affinity for full-bosomed women: "Every bosom is a provocation, every bottom a challenge."

On the one hand, my intent in "I Am a Chauvinist" was very serious. But, on the other hand, it was an ironic provocation directed against the ever-increasing proliferation of "softies"–men who spend their days preoccupied with questioning gender roles. They demonstrate their solidarity with the women's movement by squatting down to pee. In Germany, one would be well-advised to furnish every bit of satire with an instruction manual to avoid risking insurrection on the part of secondary school counselors, be they certified or not. In this case not only did dozens of *Konkret* readers–mostly men–run amok in a letter-writing frenzy (never once have I received such massive response to a "political" essay), but even a left-wing referee raised his voice to slap me on the wrist for my lack of consciousness. Just one month later, Hermann P. Piwitt assured the readers of *Konkret* that he had "nothing against tits and ass [either], who doesn't get a rise out of it?" But then he proceeded to chastise me for my "typically male" attributes: "High-handed arrogance and contempt for the sexual partner whose flesh is the only thing of interest." Piwitt put my name together in the same sentence with the poet Bukowski's (". . . pretty much a scumbag"). I'd have been flattered if he hadn't placed the infamous serial

killer Fritz Honka from Hamburg third in his lineup of horror figures, following Broder and Bukowski. *En passant* Piwitt addressed the question of which
"Weltanschauung" might have "messed up Broder so badly" and quickly arrived at "a notoriously patriarchal, that is to say, Jewish upbringing. . . ."

It would be futile to correct Piwitt *factually* and point out that the Jewish
upbringing, which he sees as the cause of my Chauvinism, is by no means
"notoriously patriarchal," but rather dominated by the mother. In the Jewish family, the father celebrates the prayers, but aside from that, he doesn't
have much say. Accordingly, every Jewish boy with any lasting regard for his
upbringing runs about his entire life with an Oedipus complex. It's not the
issue here to fill the gap in Piwittician knowledge. Piwitt had no intent of
making a statement about Jewish upbringing. Rather, he sought to hold some
"Jewish" characteristic responsible for one of my behaviors that didn't suit
him—whatever the cost.

The anti-Semitic syndrome is completely independent of its object. It is not
the Jew's behavior that counts but rather the anti-Semite's need to put a negative twist on whatever a Jew does. And that is why an anti-Semite will *always*
find *something* to sink his claws into. Years ago, Klaus Rainer Röhl accomplished something extraordinary in this regard. In a snide remark published
in an op-ed piece about Henry Kissinger, he wrote that Kissinger's outstand-
ing physical constitution could be traced back to a "several-thousand-year-long
healthy, kosher diet": especially "garlic." Röhl, an Elbchaussee Street snob, had
no idea that garlic doesn't even have anything to do with kosher diet, but at
the mere mention of a Jew, the anti-Semite reacts like Pavlov's dog to a bell,
and the smell (or better: stench) of garlic goes straight up his angular, Aryan
nose. I consider such reactions particularly telling because of the vegetative
process they entail; when the id triumphs over the ego, then even the most
enlightened intellectual is at a loss with regard to his own consciousness. He
stumbles into a snare of his own making, but one that nevertheless escapes
his eye.

During the Pope's visit to the Federal Republic, *Emma*, the "magazine by and
for women," published an open letter to the itinerate representative of the Catholic church. The letter concerned itself with the sins the Catholic church has
committed against women. Suddenly, in the middle of this open letter: "If Christians have any one thing to learn from the Talmud, it is this prayer of thanks-
giving: 'Blessed art Thou, O Lord our God, who hast not made me a woman.'"

### Subliminal Label Scam

This interjection follows the same logic and ill-logic of Piwittician "Jewish
upbringing" or the Röhlcian "kosher diet." This citation is not from the Tal-

mud but from a morning prayer for Jewish men. Misquoting a source can happen, but how does this author arrive at the Talmud of all things? The Talmud has always played a central role in the anti-Semitic platform. From the perspective of Jew-haters it is, so to speak, the cardinal sourcebook of Jewish vulgarities. If you were to assemble all that is attributed to the Talmud, the result would be a work that far exceeds the scope of the *Encyclopedia Britannica*. In all likelihood, the woman who penned this letter once heard something negative about the Talmud and has associated it with Jewish misogyny ever since. As if there are not enough examples of discrimination against women in the Catholic church, from the witch persecutions to the cult of the Virgin Mary, she has to take recourse to a Jewish exemplar–and one that doesn't even hold up under the burden of proof.

What I'd like to know now is how non-Jewish men are initiated into their Chauvinism and women-hating, since they have had neither the benefit of a patriarchal Jewish upbringing nor of thanking God every day for not having made them women.

You hold the Jews accountable not only for everything possible but also for every possible impropriety. You simply cannot let up on the Jews. The fact that the Enlightenment, the Labor movement, and any and all attempts at assimilation failed to avert the atrocities of Auschwitz doesn't even faze you. And the fact that you are compelled to concern yourselves with us again today certainly has more to do with the Jews than it does with you. You don't even realize that, like a train stuck in the mud and gravel, you proceed from precisely the same station where your parents were forced to stop in their thwarted efforts to extirpate Jewry from the world. Now you pursue the Final Solution to the Jewish Question along ideological lines. Like all anti-Semites before you, your primary concern is this: the Jews should stop being Jews, only then can you accept them.

And if you think you are not anti-Semites just because you don't define yourselves as such, then let me tell you this: it wouldn't be the first time that the content claims listed on the label didn't quite jibe with what was actually in the package.

Your label scam could be subconscious, but that doesn't speak against its existence. On the contrary, it speaks for the great efficacy of what you have internalized. Your parents have done such a thorough job that your anti-Semitic potential wanders, so to speak, like a vagabond in a vacuum. Indeed, where should it take hold, now that Hermann Tietz (Hertie), Ullstein, and Mosse have been Aryanized and, unfortunately, it's clear that even Iwan Herstatt isn't a Jew?[6] The few Jewish real estate moguls and speculators who catch your eye serve your purposes only briefly.

But thank God there is still the Über-Jew, the State of Israel, which you fret over with bitter tenacity as though you had nothing better to do. Your anti-Zionism is nothing more than a souped up, left-wing variant of anti-Semitism: the same logic, the same methodology, the same vocabulary, only with "Zionist" standing in for "Jew." And nothing has really changed. I needn't analyze the news coverage on Israel in the *UZ*, the *Rote Fahne*, the *Neue*, the *taz*, and so on.[7] I needn't prove for the umpteenth time that totally different standards are applied to Israel than to non-Jews. My everyday experiences and observations alone suffice.

For example, while visiting with a nice elderly professor in Berlin, we are joined by a social worker who works with prison inmates. He introduces us.

"Are you that Broder who wants to go to Israel?"

"Yes."

"Tell me then, how can a left-winger go to Israel?"

"Good question, ma'am, I'd be happy to provide you an answer just as soon as you tell me how a Jew can live in Germany after Auschwitz."

And with that, our exchange is over. I had no desire to engage in a debate. Yet maybe I should have asked this young lady how a left-winger can stomach living in the Federal Republic without having to vomit more than he can eat day in and day out in a country that can afford to put a former SA man in the presidency, a country where countless mass murderers run free, and where the common democratic sentiment is determined by the rate of inflation. This question would undoubtedly have been unfair, because the left-wingers cannot be held responsible for the very milieu that sustains their own futility. But for a left-winger–assuming that I am one–to go to Israel is an accusation whose justification is apparently self-explanatory.

*Konkret,* a political magazine where I have published a lot of my work, printed in its November 1980 edition an advertisement for a "publishing house for holistic research" in Wobbenbüll, postal code 2251. Even from afar, this publishing house's name and program reeks of "blood and soil." Among the titles advertised: "Roland Bohlinger, racism in Israel? A lightning rod. Is Israel achieving what the Third Reich was accused of?" In a left-wing, decidedly antifascist newspaper, this is a real improvement. The Third Reich is "accused" of something. There exists, so to speak, an allegation, but the crime the Third Reich is charged with is being committed in Israel. I spoke to the *Konkret* people about this ad, and they were embarrassed by it. It "just slipped in," no one noticed, and it would not happen again. . . . All fine and good, but can someone imagine that an ad for a book about, for instance, the "Soviet genocide in Afghanistan" could also slip into the pages so unnoticed?

An evening at a bar in Hamburg, a group of journalists, writers, university people. A conversation about fascism and its consequences. A well-known left-wing theorist in the city named Oberlercher, an avowed antifascist, says: "The only thing the Jews have learned from their persecution is how to persecute others."

A few days later, at a locale in Göttingen, this time a group of liberal lawyers, among them several liberal-minded judges. A discussion about the role played by the judiciary in the Third Reich prompts one of them to comment on the TV miniseries *Holocaust.* "I can still remember well the final scene," he said, "the younger son of the family Weiss says to his girlfriend: 'We are going to Palestine now.' And then she says: 'But there are already people there.' He says: 'Well, then they're just going to have to make room,' and ever since then, the Israelis have been doing the same thing to the Arabs that the Nazis did to the Jews." A man from Freisler's Heirs and Co. saw the Holocaust movie, and the scene that best stands out in his memory is one that he uses to equate the Jews with the Nazis.[8] Beyond that, the film apparently left him unimpressed.

I can imagine how you arrive at this obscene analogy: "The Israelis are the Nazis of the Middle East" and "the Palestinians are the Jews of Israel." This is a diversionary tactic designed to bring you historical and psychological relief. Not that you feel any sense of guilt toward the Jews. Why should you? *You* haven't touched a hair on a single Jew's head. Still, you harbor a certain sense of uneasiness–there is something not quite right about your parents.

Most of you have never confronted your parents about their past. This was something families didn't talk about, and when you did ask questions, you were forbidden from doing so. You never got an answer, and if you did, it was at best something like this: "We knew nothing" or "What could we have done anyway?"

And it could be that your father didn't spend those years he doesn't talk about on the front busting Russian tanks, but rather in the Einsatzgruppen at Warthegau cleansing the country of Jews and Gypsies behind Germany's frontlines. It could be that the dress your mother is wearing in that pristine picture from 1942 once belonged to a Jewish woman who wasn't allowed to take it with her to Auschwitz. And if indeed your father really was "only" on the front (don't forget that the concentration camps could only work as long as the front was held) and your mother had sewn the dress herself, at least they owe you an explanation about what they were *thinking* when the Cohns and Blums next door suddenly disappeared.

I know, you don't have it easy with such a burden at your back. Unfortunately, we, the children of the persecuted, are in a better position. And so you lighten your load by projecting the confrontation you never had, or never could have, with your parents onto your parents' victims. It works: the Jews are the Nazis, the Palestinians are victims of Jews, and your parents get off scot-free (as do you). They have, so to speak, nothing to work on themselves. You can again look them in the face, because now you know where the Nazis who never existed in Germany are.

## Boundless Arrogance

But that's not all. Beyond the bounds of your own familial conflicts lies something else I have already mentioned: who among you didn't hear, as a child, horror stories about "the Jew" who is at fault for everything? For capitalism, for communism, for inflation, unemployment, high interest rates, low interest rates, pornography, the war, the Schandfriede[9]–for everything the anti-Semite can't cope with and for which a scapegoat is needed. You just can't do without this scapegoat. You need him like an addict needs his fix, and no act of will nor label scam ("We have nothing against Jews, only against Zionists") offers relief. All that will help is a painful withdrawal treatment, but you've never gotten around to that because, just like your parents, you suffer from an inability to mourn. Instead you absolve yourselves from any responsibility for German history: "I didn't stick no Jew in the KZ; I didn't shoot no Poles. . . ."

Your Jew of today is the State of Israel. Just as your parents thought they'd be better off without Jews, you think that without Israel there would be no conflicts in the Middle East. There isn't a single Arab country that is not in permanent conflict with at least one other country in that region: Egypt with Libya, Libya with Tunisia, Algeria with Morocco, Morocco with Mauritania, Jordan with Syria, Syria with Iraq, Iraq with Kuwait, South Yemen with North Yemen. But for you Israel is the only troublemaker, the only obstacle to peace.

I am not saying Israel is beyond criticism. Israel's stupid, nearsighted, and sometimes catastrophic politics must be criticized. But who is it that stands up in outrage over Israel? Over the settlement policy, over the violation of human rights in the occupied territories, over the social discrimination against Israel's Arabs? They're the same people who approve of the Soviet occupation of Afghanistan, which allegedly has threatened the stability of Soviet Union, the same people who don't even know that Tibet has been occupied by China, who regard Pol-Pot's terrorist regime in Cambodia as a revolutionary people's government and ignore more than three million dead. They are the same ones who call Begin a terrorist, who do the honors before each despot, regardless of whether it is Idi Amin, Khadafy, or Khomeini, as long as he decorates himself with the "anti-imperialist" label. They are the same ones who don't give a damn about how the Kurds in Turkey are slowly but surely culturally cleansed, and how people are massacred by the hundreds in Iran and Iraq, the same ones who haven't heard a word about the genocide in Ethiopia and who overlook the ongoing "special handling" of the Gypsies in the Federal Republic.

But just who do you think you are? What is the source of your arrogance? Half the day you busy yourselves with churning out platitudes, the other half with finding the proper "assessments." None of these political debacles makes you older or wiser. The development in China took you completely by surprise. You didn't have time to revise your eternally valid standpoints as quickly as the *Beijing People's Daily* changed course. You were dumbfounded by the war between Iraqi and Persian revolutionaries. You have no idea how to react to the introduction of preventative internment in India and racial unrest there, which costs thousands of lives. That homosexuals, adulteresses, and prostitutes in Iran are murdered by the government doesn't concern you in the least.

Your free-floating potential for sympathy toward the people of the Third World wanders from continent to continent, settling sometimes here for a while, sometimes there. At present it is El Salvador, last year it was Rhodesia, the year before that it was Timor. And by the time bell bottoms have gone out of fashion in spring, you will again discover something new for revolutionary deployment in remote countries, maybe a liberation front that will liberate the Antarctic from the polar ice cap.

In your changing repertoire there is one hit that always goes over well: Palestine. No other piece of land is dearer to you; no other people nearer your heart; no conflict pushes your buttons more than this. Your interest in Palestinians can be attributed to one thing alone: it is the Jews who are oppressing them. That is all that matters. It is the motor driving you; otherwise you would not waste a single thought on the Palestinians. They just provide the stage set for you to put on your anti-Semitic programs. This too can be proven.

Not a single left-winger was incensed by the fact that the people who conducted the "selection" of Jewish passengers at Entebbe were young Germans, children of the post-generation. You didn't get upset until an Israeli commando released the hostages. And then you sent condolences–by telegram–to "His Excellence Idi Amin" and severely condemned the "violation of the sovereignty of Uganda," as if "state sovereignty" were something sacred to left-wingers. Violation of state sovereignty was nonetheless unimportant to you when a German terrorist commando attacked an FRG embassy in Stockholm.

### Indifference to Truth

These are just newer and newer variations of the same old game you're playing. Jews are afforded less latitude, but more is expected of them. They're expected to let themselves be beaten and bullied. At best, they're allowed to complain about it, never to retaliate. And when Jews behave the same way others always have, you get your hackles up. You just can't stand for it, whether it's a Jewish property owner in Frankfurt or an Israeli commando enterprise in Africa.

When Brigitte Schulz and Thomas Reuter were kidnapped by the Israeli secret service in Kenya and detained in Israel, it was an awful thing beyond the pale of justice and law, regardless of whether the two Germans had actually attempted to shoot down the El Al plane or not. You ran off at the mouth, foaming with rage at this "Zionist coup." But when news was released about at least two dozen Germans, mostly development aid volunteers, who disappeared without a trace in Argentina, when Elisabeth Käsemann, a clergyman's daughter, was murdered at the hands of government agencies in Argentina, your reactions—compared with Schulz/Reuter in Israel—were moderate. Your rage, after all, wasn't directed at Jews. We've been through all this before: whenever a child turned up missing in Russia or Poland during Passover, it was clear to everyone—once again, the Jews needed Christians' blood to bake Passover bread. There often followed a pogrom. Afterward, the Christian assassins were always terribly disappointed when a child assumed to have been "butchered" according to kosher rites showed up, or when it turned out that an Aryan perpetrator was responsible for the child's disappearance. Even today, tales about ritual murder are more credible than official party statements in Poland.

On Christmas Eve 1980, I listened to the news on WDR 2, the state-sponsored television and radio station in Cologne. Headlines from Rome: "In Pope John Paul II's opinion, Christians and Muslims are obligated to cooperate in order to attain freedom for Jerusalem and return the Holy City to all religious groups." I won't go into details about actions taken by the institution the Pope personifies in the interest of peace and of putting an end to the genocide against the Jews between Christmas Eve of 1939 and Christmas Eve of 1944. I just want to remind you, in all modesty, that, up until the Six-Day War in 1967, not a single Pope had ever called for opening the "Holy City to all religious groups." That's because, until then, the Jews were the only religious group with restricted access to their sacred sites. Today, though—under Jewish sovereignty—Jerusalem is open to followers of all faiths, so of course the supreme Shepherd of the Catholic church feels compelled to campaign for the attainment of "freedom for Jerusalem." The worst part about it: no one is outraged by it; there is no outcry.

*Ressentiment* against the Jews almost seems to be as fundamental an anthropological constant as hunger and the sex drive. In any case, it is the least common denominator in the Occident—the one thing just about everyone from the

Vatican to the Kremlin can agree upon. At least in this regard, you are right in step with the rhythm of Herr Karol Wojtyla. And you have something else in common with him: total indifference to the facts. The tales of ritual murder were as difficult to refute with facts as was that classic work of anti-Semitic propaganda, *The Protocols of the Elders of Zion*, penned by the czarist secret police. And, when it suits your purpose, you're just as loose with your handling of facts.

You frankly don't have a clue about anything, yet always a pat answer for everything. You are oblivious to the fact that Israel took in the same number of Jews from Arab countries as Arabs who fled Palestine in 1948. You talk about Palestine and what you have in mind is the small coastal strip, the territory that encompasses Israel, Gaza, and the West Bank. What you don't know is that, historically, the territory east of Jordan once belonged to Palestine, and it wasn't until 1922 that the Brits "ceded" it to the Hashemit Dynasty from which King Hussein descended. You don't know either that King Hussein's grandfather, Abdullah, advocated for a peaceful coexistence between Jews and Arabs and was assassinated by Arab terrorists in 1947 because of it. You reject everything that could rattle your prefabricated resentment.

The January 1981 issue of *Emma* appeared on the market as I was writing this essay. On the back cover there was a preview of "the next *Emma*." Among other things, there was an announcement for the following topic: "Palestine: Ingrid Strobl was there." Where was Frau Strobl? In *Palestine*. She flew from Frankfurt to Tel Aviv, drove from there across Israel to Jerusalem, and met her PLO friends in East Jerusalem. For *Emma*, Israel no longer exists–the second phase of the Final Solution is obviously already a done deal and only a matter of time.

I asked Alice Schwarzer what she was thinking when she made this announcement. She told me she hadn't had anything particular in mind–apologizing for something based on thoughtlessness without realizing that it's the very thoughtlessness of it that makes it so bad. How self-evident the unthinking annihilation of Jewish existence has again become–so self-evident, in fact, that it doesn't even enter your mind.

Meanwhile, Frau Strobl, back from Palestine, reports from Cologne that the Jews have no business in Palestine. It's absolutely silly to claim that just because some Hebrew tribes had once lived there two thousand years ago. . . .

I didn't even begin to attempt an explanation of the historical, religious, and metaphysical ties that she might not be able to understand but which play an important role for others. I took recourse to a simpler line of argumentation and said that for two thousand years we tried without the formal structure of a state and experienced plenty of difficulties. Frau Strobl, a Doctor of Philosophy, replied that we should try to establish the Jewish state somewhere else, maybe in Bavaria, but we should leave the Palestinians alone; they hadn't done us any harm.

There's something to that statement. As a matter of fact, Palestinians are footing a part of the bill, for which Frau Strobl's parents, *pars pro toto*, are responsible. But Frau Strobl keeps silent on this front; instead, she recommends that the Israelis haul their asses out of Palestine.

At least Frau Strobl is honest about her resentment. She concedes that, for her, it's not about a few occupied territories, the West Bank, Gaza, the Goland Heights; for her, Israel would still be an occupying country that should be dissolved, even if it limits itself to the city of Tel Aviv. She is not concerned about a just balance in the Middle East, not concerned that both sides, Israelis and Arabs, should compromise and arrive at some sort of modus vivendi, lest they all go down together. She is concerned, like many German left-wingers, about the principle: there should be no Jewish state. This is the second leg on the road to the Final Solution, and your ticket's already been booked in advance.

While your mothers and fathers have moved beyond Auschwitz to daily life, as if the whole thing were nothing more than a rain-soaked summer, while German courts debate the "authenticity" of Anne Frank's diary and the propaganda of the right wing declares not only the diary but the whole Jewish persecution a fraud, while the youth born during Ludwig Erhard's reign make silly jokes about how many Jews fit into a VW ashtray,[10] you agitate for the dissolution of the State of Israel, and continue, though with different means, the work of Adolf Eichmann. Whoever denies the right of a Jewish state's existence forty years after Auschwitz and–though not altogether directly–pursues a political solution that would lead to the destruction of Israel should know the goal of his campaign. And he should also know that he will not be able to wash his hands in innocence if. . . .

I'm at the end: at the end of this article, at the end of my rage. And I'm also finished with you, my left-wing friends. I won't suffer your stupidity anymore; I won't bother to tell you what your parents kept secret anymore; I won't criticize you or enlighten you, I won't be your token antifascist Jew–I don't want anything to do with you.

This is the first essay I have written from the us-and-them perspective. Even one year ago, I wouldn't have done such a thing. But there's no other way, even though I know I may be doing some of you a disservice: the one Uwe or another, the Manfred and the Detlef, the Barbara and the Hilde, the Peter and the Hanno, the Günter and the Gerhard, and certainly some others whose names don't occur to me now.

Back in the old days, every German knew at least one fine, upstanding Jew. Today, I know a couple of fine, upstanding Germans.

So it is that times change.

*Translated by Qinna Shen*

## NOTES

All notes are by the translator except where indicated.

1. In the beginning of 1981 the young Jewish journalist Henryk Broder left Germany—his adopted country. Yet before he departed for Israel, he wrote an open letter to his "left-wing friends." This was his way of settling the account with an anti-Zionist sentiment that masks ancient anti-Semitic instincts with progressive slogans—it is a document of outrage and of resignation. (*Spiegel* editor's note.)

2. When the RAF member Ulrike Meinhof was found dead in her cell in Stammheim prison near Stuttgart, the death was officially reported as "suicide," but leftist circles generally assumed she had been executed.

3. Broder refers here to postwar "show trials" against high-ranking Jews in the Communist party that led to the execution of many Eastern European Jews. Laszlo Rajk, the Hungarian foreign minister, was executed in 1949 on charges of anti-Sovietism and Titoism; Rudolf Slansky, the secretary of the Czechoslovakian Communist party, was executed in 1952 on charges of "bourgeois nationalism." The 1953 Physicians' Trial was Stalin's final anti-Semitic campaign against Jewish doctors shortly before his death in March 1953.

4. *Das Reich* was a widely circulated weekly during the Nazi period; *Der Stürmer* is the notorious Nazi publication that was edited by Julius Streicher from 1923–45.

5. The reference is to Gerhard Zwerenz's 1971 novel, *Die Erde ist so unbewohnbar wie der Mond* (Earth is as uninhabitable as the moon); the novel was used as the basis for Rainer Werner Fassbinder's 1973 film *The Trash, The City, and Death.*

6. Hertie Konzern is a large department store chain founded by Hermann Tietz; Ullstein is the name of a publishing house in Berlin, founded in 1877; Mosse is an advertising firm.

7. *UZ* (*Unsere Zeitung*) is the central organ of the German Communist party (DKP); *Die Rote Fahne* was the central organ of the KPD; *Die Neue* was an independent left-wing weekly newspaper; *die taz* (*die tageszeitung*) is the left-wing Berlin daily.

8. Dr. Roland Freisler (1893–1945) was a notorious cruel judge in Nazi Germany.

9. The term the National Socialists used to describe the conditions of "peace" prevailing after the Treaty of Versailles (June 28, 1919).

10. Ludwig Erhard, a CDU/CSU politician, held high cabinet posts under Adenauer and was later elected to vice chancellor and minister of finance. Following Adenauer's 1963 resignation, Erhard became chancellor. He resigned in 1966. He continued to play a significant role in right-wing politics to the time of his death in 1977.

After about fifteen years' conscious public political writing, I no longer see any sense in continuing this work. It's not that I've been prevented from doing my work; I haven't encountered any more difficulties than others—rather, fewer. When it came down to it, the solidarity was there. If I nevertheless quit involving myself in matters that concern this Republic, there are three reasons for it:

- I won't continue these surrogate battles, working myself up daily over things that the majority of Germans don't get worked up over. In the long run, history cannot be "mastered" predominately on the backs of its victims.
- I have many personal friends here but as good as no political allies. The right-wing "philo-Semites" like Strauß and Springer were always out of the question for me as allies, since I cannot ally myself with reactionaries just because they happen to have fallen in love with the Jews for once.
- Nor can I join the ranks of the left wing in the fight against reactionaries and repression as long as they only accept me when my Jewishness—as rudimentary as it is—doesn't strike them as troublesome. The belief in the historical and political necessity for a Jewish state is one unshakeable, fundamental aspect of that Jewishness.

Left-wingers in this country have devoted considerable thought to a great number of things: the role of the Left in a constitutional state, of women in men's society, of workers in capitalism, and of art in commerce. But to ask how Jews in the post-Auschwitz landscape must feel about the anti-Zionist uproar on the Left—that doesn't even enter their minds.

*Translated by Qinna Shen*

3

## HEIMAT? —
## NO THANKS!

Whenever I approach a new topic, I begin by looking up the word and its associations in the dictionary. In the unabridged paperback edition of *Mayer's
Lexikon*, I found the following: "*Heimat* ['homeland' or 'native country']:–a
territorial unit experienced subjectively by individuals or collective groups,
tribes, populations, or nations who identify themselves as sharing a certain
feeling of connectedness." The dictionary also provided several variations of
*Heimat*, among them *Heimatkunst* (regional arts and crafts), the *Heimatmu-
seum* (museum of local history and culture), the *Heimatschein* (certificate of
prescribed nationality), a peculiarity of Swiss municipal law, and *heimatlose
Ausländer* (homeless foreigners), who apparently are hit hard twice, first as
Ausländer (foreigners) and second as *heimatlos* (persons without a homeland
or a home). Then there is the *Heimatschutztruppe* (homeland security force),
a subdivision of the territorial forces of the Bundeswehr (German federal
armed forces), which is supposed to protect the homeland in states of emergency. This, of course, automatically raises the question as to what the exact

responsibilities of the regular army are if war is perceived per se as a condition of defense.

Already, our first casual encounter with the word *Heimat* produces a diverse set of terms that leads us deeper into abstractions than toward the clarity we initially sought. I find the word and its connotations altogether suspect. To me, it has about it an air that is stuffy, stifling, and stale. It smells of homesteads, bootleg schnapps, and barn stables. And whether I want to or not, I connect the term with dirndls, half-timber cottages, and the big-game hunts of the local rifle association. In other words, *Heimat* has rural connotations for me. From an objective point of view, my hunches may be incorrect, and yet these free associations are by no means arbitrary. I reproduce images and impressions *from a* Heimat that have been passed down to me *as* Heimat.

It's no accident that *Heimatkunst* (regional arts and crafts) and *Heimatdichtung* (local color literature) aren't born in big cities and metropolises and that both terms sound as robust and rustic as *Hausschlachtung* (whole-stock cattle ranches) and *freiwillige Feuerwehr* (volunteer fire departments). When speaking of a Heimat writer from Munich or Berlin, the emphasis ought to be placed on the author's more or less coincidental urban circumstance, not reduced to the most obvious—that is, to his dialect, the vernacular in which he writes, or the specific section of town in which he lives. In this sense, the big-city Heimat artist is a contradictory concept and, at the same time, an attempt to pump a little heartland into an area ordinarily associated with urban decadence and alienation. It is the desire, even in the middle of an asphalt jungle, to recover a small plot of pastoral idyll.

Whether in the chronicles of Edgar Reitz or the popular German soap opera set in the Black Forest region, the gist of *Heimat* is conveyed when characters define themselves above and apart from their dwellings. These figures did not end up where they are for no reason, and if they have, each wants to belong, to be accepted within the community. Furthermore, they did not make the move in order to improve their standard of living. Quite to the contrary. Each has held true to his Heimat, has often taken on hardships and difficulties in order to avoid fleeing his homeland. As a result, one could compare the notion of *Heimat* to a Russian doll within a doll within a doll. It can be broken into smaller and smaller parts. A German might find himself lost in France. A native of the Rhine might feel like a stranger in Hamburg and a person from Cologne who grew up along the west bank of the Rhine might speak of the Rhine's east bank, the so-called Schääl Sick, as if he were referring to the dark side of the moon. I hardly know anyone who lives in the same place he was born. Such people might exist, but it happens that in my surroundings this is more often the exception than the rule. This being the case, I could say that I live exclusively among *Heimatlose* (those without a homeland) and *Heimatvertriebene* (those driven from their homeland), who nonetheless have laid claim to a chosen Heimat, a Heimat of choice.

I was born in Katowice shortly after the war in 1946. Both of my parents had been in concentration camps and belonged to the less than ten percent of Polish Jews who survived the so-called Holocaust—a remarkable coincidence, when I consider that my older sister, hidden under a mattress by a poor Catholic family in Poland, survived as well. In 1957, twelve years after the war, my family moved to the Federal Republic of Germany by way of Vienna. My sister, a Zionist at the time, was the only one who moved to Israel. For me, our leaving Poland was merely a move and nothing more. At the age of eleven, I had developed neither a love of my homeland nor any further emotional bonds. The only thing that made parting painful and difficult was that I could not take along my wiener dog, and he was given away to strangers instead. For my parents, the circumstances were a little different. My father came from Galicia, my mother from Krakow. Both were shaped by the places where they spent their childhoods—he by the Shtetl, and she by the imperial and royal atmosphere in the colonies of the House of Habsburg. But with the coming of the war, the Shtetl, my father's birthplace, was destroyed, and Krakow had long since ceased to be a suburb of Vienna.

Nonetheless, it wasn't easy for my parents to leave Poland. The unabated anti-Semitism in Poland certainly helped facilitate their decision to move to Germany. Ultimately, however, they relocated for linguistic reasons. Both grew up with the German language and did not want to live in a country in which they could not communicate freely. In Israel, they would have encountered not only Polish but Russian, German, and Yiddish spoken side by side. There wouldn't have been a language barrier, but Israel after all was a country somewhere in Asia with a miserable climate and, well, so many Jews in one place, that didn't have to be. . . .

The first years in Germany passed relatively smoothly. I can't say we found a home away from home there. No, Germany was and remained a transitional solution, a trial of unforeseeable duration. And yet I don't believe our situation was much different from that of a family who moved from East Prussia to the Rhineland, for example. When Carnival broke loose in Cologne, an event that took place as faithfully as Easter and was equally unavoidable, I felt like Captain Cook traveling as a visitor to some strange, savage tribe amidst natives who could all be charmingly funny on command, suddenly swaying to and fro like autistic children and laughing over jokes I never once understood.

During Carnival, especially during the so-called Tollen Tage (crazy days), which can be taken literally in Cologne, I knew: *I'm not at home here. There are worlds between me and these savages.*

When I returned to Cologne from a trip, however, and the towers of the Dome emerged on the horizon; when, after several hours of driving on the Autobahn, I crossed the Rhine and saw before me the original old part of town that was kitschy and quaint as a postcard from a distance, I had the feeling that I was going home. A sympathetic nerve was touched, and a warm sentiment stirred. In that ambivalent state, I looked forward to returning to the place where I didn't feel at home at all. Suddenly, it became livable, especially because Cologne held claim to one notable geographic advantage: it was close to Holland. And so a trip to the neighboring city of Maastricht could satisfy two desires at once: the need to get away, and the need to return. Without my being aware, the whole affair was a Jewish joke put into practice, whereby the punch line went: "the best part of the journey is getting there." Whenever possible, I was always on my way somewhere. It wasn't just Wanderlust that drove me but the desire to change locations, the love of motion itself. One could assume that this is a characteristically Jewish trait. If there really is something like a spirit of the masses, a collective character, a pattern of behavior that distinguishes one group of people, then a nomadic slant belongs to the set of common attributes among Jews. The Exodus from Egypt and the forty-year journey through the desert occupy a central position in Jewish consciousness. This historic event has been commemorated annually in Passover festivities for the past three thousand years as if it occurred just yesterday. Moving away, relocating, emigrating, giving up a home, looking for a new one—these are normal experiences in Jewish life, experiences that have repeated themselves persistently throughout history. Ahasver, the Wandering Jew, is constantly astray. But the notion of the Jew as pariah is *not* a Semitic one: it has its roots in the New Testament and since the seventeenth century has been stylized in numerous writings and legends as a sinister figure of horror.

It is moot to argue whether a person's character determines his circumstances in life or a person's circumstances in life determine his character. At any rate, Jews have always had a fairly loose relationship to fixed dwellings, even in regions where they have lived for extended periods of time. Living with the possibility that any day a pogrom could break loose forces one to develop certain habits to accommodate immanent danger. Ideally, everything was mobile. A small sack of gold or diamonds was easier to carry than a house or a piece of property. Material objects without practical value were not important. A bed, a dresser, a table did not have to be beautiful, only useful. Studies were important. Food was important. Close family ties were important. The lack of aesthetic training, the residual effects of which can still be observed in every other Israeli apartment, and the emphasis on skills like abstract thinking and mental dexterity that one can apply anywhere were the direct cause and result of a mobility that is seen as classically Jewish and also serves as a negative cliché to support the presumption that Jews lack a Heimat and are uprooted: that is, it reinforces the image of the Ahasver, or Wandering Jew. *Heimat*–homeland–was never in itself a territorial term.

Heinrich Heine was the first to speak of a "portable fatherland," whereby he included religious heritage, tradition, and overall way of life. The Jews always had with them what they required from their Heimat–if need be, contained in a small emergency pack. Whether in Lvov or Long Island, the Sabbath candles were always lit Friday at sundown. During Passover matzo was served everywhere, and during Yom Kippur one fasted. The notion that *Heimat* also referred to a plot of land emerged in Jewish culture only during the second half of the previous century at a time much later than for other populations.

"Let the sovereignty be granted us over a portion of the globe large enough to satisfy the rightful requirements of a nation; the rest we shall manage for ourselves," wrote Theodor Herzl in his 1896 work, *The Jewish State.*[1] Nowhere was his proposal met with such hostility as in the Jewish community, which fought tooth and nail against the idea of being transformed from a cultural nation into a territorial nation. At that particular point, the Jews had several options open to them. An orthodox minority acted as if the Enlightenment and emancipation never took place and attempted to carry on with their lives as they had in the ghetto even after the ghetto walls fell. Pursuant to the Jewish Question, a secular minority saw at hand not a social or religious but a national question that should be resolved politically in consultation with civilized nations, as proposed by Herzl. The Zionist movement was intended to serve this purpose. The majority of Jews in Germany sought a symbiosis between Jewishness and Germanness. The latter constituted the "German citizens of Jewish faith," who wished to differ from their Christian compatriots only in religious practice. In other words, at the beginning of this century, Jews in Germany could decide between three definitions of *Heimat:* the spiritual homeland of a portable fatherland, the national homeland of Zionism, and the "symbiotic" homeland of integration.

The turn that history took is well known to us all. All efforts at assimilation proved futile. The desperate struggle for recognition as good Germans was a prelude to the greatest catastrophe of Jewish history.

Now when asked whether I have a Heimat and, if so, where, I answer in the best Jewish custom–evasively. I believe I do have a Heimat, but I cannot localize it. It is the scent of gefilte fish and latkes, the taste of *borscht* and fried herring. It is the melody of *Hatikva* and the sound of cosmopolitanism, but only when it is sung in Yiddish by the old residents in Tel Aviv on May 1. It is a night in the Marx Brothers' *Casablanca* or Ernst Lubitsch's *To Be or Not to Be*. It is Karl Kraus's torch and Theodor Lessing's autobiography. It is a spot on the Aussenalster in Hamburg, a small stoop in the old harbor of Jaffo, and the Leidseplein in Amsterdam. And isn't that enough?

The greatest problem with *Heimat* seems to me that one is expected to choose one. It would be better to simply have none at all. Or better yet: to have many all at once.

*Translated by Andrea Scott*

**NOTE**

1. Theodor Herzl, *The Jewish State,* trans. Jakob Alkow (New York: Dover Publications, 1988), 92.

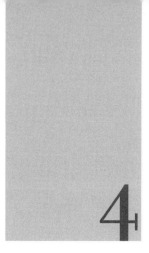

## DON'T FORGET

## TO DIFFERENTIATE!

I recently took part in a public discussion where one participant spoke of the "murder of millions" of Jews. In response, a young woman from the audience spoke up, saying that one must be very exact about these matters and clearly differentiate. From a legal point of view, she protested, it could have been, at least in part, a matter of manslaughter. At that point, I yelled out, "Indeed, it could have been a simple matter of bodily injury resulting in death!"–and the young woman called back, "Yes, that too."

Differentiation seems to have become the dictate of the hour, and all over the country people are straining to differentiate as precisely as possible. A police officer is charged with assault. That he struck his victim is without a doubt. One witness says, with a fist. Another witness says, with an open hand. In this case, differentiation between the testimonies leads to an acquittal. A diplomat from the Office of Foreign Affairs gives a speech commemorating Reichskristallnacht during which he says that the "implementation" of the pogrom was "assigned to the SA and, partially, to the SS," whereby "the latter was only grudgingly prepared to dirty its hands in the matter." The speech was printed by a newspaper that ruminated in their feuilleton on "how terribly easily the Jews let themselves be forced into the role of victim, to the point of sheer obscene collaboration with the perpetrators. . . ."

A precise observation, and properly differentiated. On the one hand, a "begrudging" SS, reluctant to dirty its hands, and, on the other, those Jews just hot to trot in collaboration, enthusiastically accommodating their persecutors. This differentiation, too, was long overdue.

A new innocence and fresh shamelessness follows general demands for differentiation. This strategy separates itself from its predecessors insofar as it supplants a defensive denial ("What has all that crap got to do with me?") with a readiness to tackle those issues that don't concern one personally—just as long as they are properly differentiated, of course.

During a reading at a southern German university I said—among other things—that, at least since Auschwitz, it is up to the Jews to determine what constitutes anti-Semitism. Afterward, one student protested my opinion, stating that the Jews could not claim "a monopoly on the definition of anti-Semitism." I considered this form of symbolic "antimonopolism" a belated postscript to the struggle against the Jewish monopolies—an effort that, for lack of Jewish bankers, publishers, and manufacturers, has taken aim against the last Jewish "monopoly," namely, the desire on the part of the Jews to decide for themselves what they consider Jew-hating. But on closer examination, her stance revealed itself to be a differentiated position that courageously unveiled a network of hidden historical connections. Taking recourse to the Jewish monopoly on defining anti-Semitism, the student instructed me on the way "the murdered are misappropriated by their legal heirs to function as an alibi for nationalism." The Holocaust is invoked as a way of "nullifying" the massacres the Jews have orchestrated since then. The protest against the misappropriation of the murdered Jews by the survivors and by future generations was an expression of genuine concern for the dignity of the dead and at the same time a sign of the careful differentiation of a delicate phenomenon: one cannot leave Jews to decide what constitutes anti-Semitism—why, they can't even reach a consensus among themselves as to who qualifies as a Jew. Or the other way around: it is much too serious an affair to entrust the Jews of all people with the task of determining the parameters of what is defined as anti-Semitism.

Whoever refutes such a differentiated position with the flat rebuttal that ultimately it should be women's place to decide what is misogynist and gay people's place to decide when they feel aggrieved and attacked has overlooked the fact that neither women nor gays have ever held a monopoly on the definition of misogyny and homophobia. At best they can join in the discussion and have their voices heard, and no more. Why should Jews be afforded a privilege that other groups in society do not have?

In an environment characterized by such clear and calculated differentiation, I'm afraid I cannot avoid owning up to a bad public gaffe. I claimed that a Frankfurt theater director had spoken about an "end of the Schonzeit" (or "grace period") in a discussion of a Fassbinder piece entitled *The Trash, the City, and Death*. He had in fact said this, but not–as I had implied–in reference to the Jews but rather with the piece itself in mind. He stated that we must concern ourselves with the work "after ten years, ten years since we pushed it aside, ten years of Schonzeit." Quite correctly, the director protested against my implication and explained (in the quiet atmosphere of a judge's chambers) that a theater piece needs a "Schonzeit" before it can be staged, that this is an old concept from the theater world, a fact to which experts would testify. Dolt that I am, I had never heard that theater pieces must be *geschont*, or "protected" by *not* putting them on. Heedless of differentiation, I had drawn the wrong conclusions. Once bitten, twice shy. Now I am working harder, and soon I will belong to those whose ability to differentiate grows each time it is tested.

*Translated by Kenneth McGill*

5

## I LOVE KARSTADT

The question "Do you love Germany?" is without doubt a *klotzkasche*–the Yiddish word for a difficult question. A *klotzkasche* can never be answered with a simple yes or no. Either answer would be insufficient and somehow tactless, as if one were to win the lottery and celebrate with an extra large order of fries, only covered in caviar instead of ketchup. A *klotzkasche* must be bandied about, mulled over with your hands clasped behind your back, and it is ultimately best answered with another question. For this particular question, the correct answer might be, "Well, should I?" Should a Polish Jew who has spent twenty-three years in Germany (wasting about half that time trying to prove to the "proper" Germans that he is the "better" German), who, despite the fact that he has lived in Israel with a German passport for the past five years, still insists on thinking, speaking, and writing in German–should this person love Germany, and, things being as they are, should he suffer under Germany's shadow? What good would that do?

Gustav Heinemann once said that he would only make love with his wife, not the state. For lack of any other resolutely sensible quotations from German politicians, this proposition has become famous. It is often quoted when the difficult relationship between the state and the individual is scrutinized for psychosexual content. Nevertheless, there are said to be people who manage to make bedfellows of their wives *and* their fatherland, if perhaps for different reasons and in different ways. The Jewish philosopher and writer Theodor Lessing, who loved Germany and whom the Nazis killed in exile in 1933, spoke about this theme with a different twist. One can, he wrote in one of his last essays, belong to two nations just as easily as one can love two women; one must only take care that "the situation does not develop into tragedy." I, for one, have always found the compromise formula "both this and that" much more appealing than the ridiculous choice between "either-or." Where others perceive a contradiction, even an antagonistic one, I see the chance to explore the multitude of possibilities.

Enthusiasm for Heimat or "homeland" in Germany has been pervasive of late. This reminds me of two old Yiddish jokes. A Jew is always traveling from one place to another. He can't stay put for long, barely has he settled in when he has to pack up again. When someone asks him what forces him to keep moving in this way, he answers, "The best part of the journey is getting there." Another Jew is traveling on a train, and at each station where the train stops, he breaks out, "Oy-vay, oy-vay, what trouble I'm in, Oy-vay, oy-vay!" His exclamations become louder from station to station, until finally one of his fellow travelers asks him what is wrong. "I got on the wrong train," answers the Jew, "and with every station the return trip gets longer."

With Heimat, I suspect, it is even worse. Since you can't get off the train, you have to at least act as if you embarked of your own free will.

Some years ago, I met a Swiss man who explained (in a single breath) why he is glad to be Swiss. "With us, the state is only there to pick up the garbage and issue passports." That was enough, it seems, to convince him that Switzerland was superior to West Germany, where the state is less a provider of services than an ideological enterprise *from* which some constantly distance themselves and *with* which others constantly claim solidarity. You could also say: the line is drawn between those who are proud to have invented the Radikalenerlaß, the ban on employment of radical teachers and civil servants in Germany, and those who are proud that it has been used against them, since otherwise no one would really believe that they are a danger to the system, let alone give official confirmation of such a fact. It seems to me that the latter are the ones who love Germany most, since they are the ones most consistently ground down and battered on behalf of their beliefs.

Is there any stronger, more convincing and conclusive evidence for the love of Germany than the suicides in Stammheim?[1] So much unrequited affection, so much readiness to sacrifice, all followed by a complete rejection of the object of desire. Like any great love story, it must have a deadly ending.

For me it was different right from the start, though through no fault of my own. I was eleven years old when I arrived in Germany. I didn't speak a word of German, and the only ambition I had was to speak this language better than the people who taught me. After four or five years, it got to the point that I could correct my teachers on the fine points of grammar. This had little to do with love; quite the opposite. I hated the school, which seemed like a dungeon, the mediocre and pompous teachers, and my fellow pupils, a pack of sycophants, opportunists, and denunciators. Graduation was a deliverance. Only the Count of Monte Cristo could have felt more free after his escape from prison. My psychosomatic complaints disappeared, I grew a beard, gained weight, and took a vow: Never another exam!

In school I learned two lessons that would serve me for life. The first: you have to work awfully hard, or at least act like you are, because anything done lightly won't be taken seriously. If I turned in an in-class composition after a single hour and went home, I would get for the work a "satisfactory" (at best!). But if I was done in an hour and nevertheless spent the rest of the class staring intently out the window, the same piece of writing would get a "very good." The second lesson: you can never do anything for your own sake. A person must be noble, helpful, and mendacious and must hide his egoism behind the facade of community spirit, conscientiousness, and altruism. Cleverly position yourself . . . this is how you get ahead. Our teachers, for instance, had almost all given up promising careers as artists, scientists, decatheletes, and writers in order to bring knowledge of gothic architecture, photosynthesis, Latin grammar, and the correct pronunciation of "th" in English to contrary and ungrateful students. The regret they felt on contemplation of all those careers they passed by in the service of public education was surpassed only by the absorption they showed upon contemplation of the vested interest accumulating in their pension fund.

I found this all rather revolting and reacted like a peacock locked in a cage with a bunch of ugly ducklings. The plumage I fanned out behind me could not be big enough. I had calling cards printed, presenting myself as "one of the last true geniuses of our time." On my stationery, at the top of the page, stood a motto I had stolen from Tucholsky, "What little I do read, I have written myself." At a time when the word "fuck" could unleash a scandal of theatrical proportion, I founded a newspaper called "POPOPO" (POp-POlitics-POrnography). Later, I published a pamphlet (BUBU) having to do solely with myself. At that time, nothing bothered me more than a demand that I be serious. But I didn't often have to reckon with such reproaches, and bit by bit a sense of accomplishment set in to fuel my self-esteem.

A public prosecutor from Cologne–one of the simplest of his kind–sent to my home a restraining order barring me from calling him "Gottlieb" or "Gottfried" or similar such inappropriate names. You see, I had constantly and intentionally called him Gottlieb, even though his real name was Klaus. Following a meeting to which one of the members had brought a piece of my stationery, a committee from West German Radio had a long discussion about whether "the Communist Broder" could at all be tolerated as a freelance writer. On the paper in question were five heads: mine followed by that of Marx, Engels, Lenin, Stalin, and Mao. The five red stylites all peered to the right, and I alone to the left. I had refrained from explaining this subtle point in a footnote.

My first police summons came when I was seventeen or eighteen. I had ordered a few brochures from the GDR (back then, it was still called the GDR or SBZ) that were sent in due order but arrived at the fourteenth (political) police precinct instead of in my mail. These brochures brought me under suspicion of treason. Although this was our first encounter, I would meet the officer who questioned me that day many times. He observed demonstrations and always seemed a bit put out by the fact that they took place exactly when he would rather be sitting at home watching sports. He did not care to accept my friendly invitations for a glass of tea, nor did he ever take me up on my offer of a ride home after the demonstration. Once he tried (putatively in self-defense) to toss me down the stairs of the station house. I've long since forgiven him. Can you really hold a touch of prison fever against a "lifer"?

I trained myself, whenever I could, to provoke people and to attract attention. None of it was for love of the country in which I lived. It was a constant rehearsal for the moment–where and when it would arrive I never knew–that the cat and mouse game would begin where I, naturally, was the mouse that always outsmarted the cat. At the same time, this was the substitute for the attention that I truly wanted. In Germany, this type of behavior is often reckoned with in drug-dealing and prostitution circles, both allowed to unfold only in certain restricted areas–like at Carnival, in the red light district, or in statements issued by Helmut Kohl. In my own immediate surroundings, this sort of stimulation was sorely lacking. It was really easy to provoke people, to anger them and force them to tip their hand. It required no effort at all; I hardly had to lift a finger.

Without my intention, things often escalated from a fart to a torchlight procession or "*vom Furz zum Fackelzug*," as it is so graphically described in the vernacular of Cologne. One day I wanted to fly from Cologne to Zurich. A tremendous hubbub began when two particularly clutzy Federal Border Police attempted to confiscate a manuscript of mine. It eventually came out that the customs officials had instructions to inspect luggage for books and printed materials. In the end, the then-sitting minister of the interior, Maihofer (a liberal), was rather worse for wear. A short visit to a criminal court and an ensuing radio commentary led to a confrontation with a Cologne judge that was to last several years. This particular man had a perverse inclination to take offense. Every one of my public accounts was met by another of his legal complaints, and each of his complaints was met by another one of my accounts. We continued to work each other up until an internal memo from the Justice Ministry surfaced in which it came out that the judge ("a man of international disrepute . . . self-justified, coarse, and merciless") seemed to regard the criminal justice system as a means for bolstering his shattered health. It was nevertheless rather late in the game that his superiors (who until then had covered up all of his deeds and misdeeds) took him out of the line of fire and placed him in a civil court, where he would have to do without the satisfaction of deciding how to fill up cells in Cologne Prison.

At the time I did not know where any of this would lead. Into the wild blue yonder, and the trip was worth the ride. In hindsight, it seems to me that I inherited a certain grumbling disposition from my father, a trait that combined with exhibitionist vanity and the typical Jewish tendency toward stubbornness. In Jewish families, outside authorities don't mean much, and the German authorities were not only suspicious from the start ("What was he doing forty years ago?"), they seemed predestined by nature to draw justified (as well as unjustified) anger towards themselves. What did not occur to me at the time, while I was being forced to contend with so many judges, police, and other representatives of the bureaucratic world, was the Janus-faced nature of my own activism. On the one hand, I wanted to be more antiauthoritarian, "cheeky," and stubborn than my first German friends, all in order to confirm the fact that I "belonged." On the other hand, I had to compensate for the confrontation with my parents that never happened.

A Jewish child born in 1946 is definitely handicapped in relation to the people who raised him. While my German friends either feared or hated their parents, I felt a constant feeling of guilt toward mine.

There was nothing there to fear or hate. This fact certainly had its advantages, but it had also had one terrible disadvantage. When I couldn't live up to their expectations, which was often the case, I never had the option of simply banging my fist on the table and yelling "stick it up your ass!" What had these poor people suffered, what had they struggled through and endured until 1945, what

kind of hope had they vested in me? I was proof that life, and not merely survival, had some meaning. Disobey them—even if the whole bagatelle amount-
ed to simply refusing to cut my hair or to go with them to Bad Kissingen!—and
they no longer knew why they survived the concentration camps. They had
survived *for my sake,* and I wasn't even prepared to go to the barber so that they
wouldn't be ashamed of my shoulder-length hair in front of the neighbors. My
"inappropriate behavior" was grotesquely disproportionate to the reaction that
it set off. Under such conditions, consequential and radical rebellion against
my parents was impossible. And if I tried it anyway, the guilt I already felt would
grow out of proportion. In such a situation, there are only two solutions: either
one starts his own family in order to pass on the pressure of the guilt he feels;
or one finds surrogates to attack, torment, and "kill" without feeling guilty. And
without knowing why, that is exactly what I have done. The struggles that I
threw myself into eased the tension between me and my parents and strength-
ened the self-confidence I felt in the face of my environment. I felt like Robin
Hood in a forest of paragraphs. The danger that I might become a Michael
Kohlhaas did not even occur to me.[2]

Even if I remember everything being better than it actually was, even if I act
like a veteran of Verdun who, looking back, seems to think that the battle was
a jolly good time full of sound and fury, I am at the same time pretty sure that
my balance is positive, that all of the little victories and defeats have done me
more good than harm. I've entertained myself and a few others, and I have
learned to stand my ground and not to give in. At the same time, I've risked
nothing substantial. I've been criminally convicted for slandering a German
judge. But these days that is worth about as much as a dueling scar was in its
day. Looking at it this way, I might have reason enough to love Germany like a
son might love his stern father . . . a man he might curse, a relationship he might
rail against, but ultimately the one thing that made him what he is. I would have,
at the very least, reason to be thankful. But instead of love or gratitude, I feel
something else. I see this country from a distance, and it astounds me.

After five years in a country that has the somewhat foolish self-image of a
European enclave in the Middle Eastern desert, I am beginning to value all
those traits I used to despise: punctuality, dependability, order. Whenever I go
to an Israeli bank or post office, I think to myself that this must be my punish-
ment for making fun of "German efficiency." Every time I have to wait in line
at the supermarket because the cashier can't find the PCU, or because she's
confused the PCU with the price, which then puts the whole computer out of
order, I wish for a moment I were in the grocery department at Karstadt's in
Cologne. And every time I come to Cologne to visit my mother, the first thing
I do is run to Karstadt and just gape: What order! What selection! What abun-

dance! The counters without end, filled with cheese and sausage and tins of all types! How tastefully presented! And how cheap! I act like East Germans do their first time in Kaufhaus des Westens on Berlin's Kurfürstendamm. After two or three days in a consumer frenzy, I begin to settle down a bit, and instead of seeing Germany as a gigantic shopping cart, I can again begin paying attention to more substantial things.

It springs to mind immediately how aware most Germans are of their responsibilities. When they are not "bothered," they are used to taking on great amounts of responsibility. Recently, I was in the Bundestag when Hans Dietrich Genscher gave a speech about "the foreigner question." He spoke about "our foreign fellow citizens" and claimed that it was the mark of responsible government to send "them" all home, that such actions lie in the best interests of the immigrants themselves—a logical flip-flop that did not elicit a peep of laughter.

The next day I took the train to Bremen. In the compartments small posters hung above the seats. One advertised Bad Salzuflen, another the Innere Mission (domestic mission), and a third read: "15 million on the run. Without home, without food, without school, without a future. Running from hunger, because their own country can no longer feed them, running from war and civil war. Running to escape servitude to a dictator or an ideology. And running from religious, racial, or ethnic oppression. On the run. . . ." It wouldn't have hurt to say who was actually running from whom, from where, and to where. But, apparently, the tiny poster was less about current information then it was a symbol for universal feelings of responsibility. Whereas the German nation was once thought to be the world's salvation, Germany was now confronted with the task of redeeming itself in the eyes of the rest of the world by constantly proclaiming to be responsible for, or at least "bothered" by, developments the world over.[5]

About the same time, I took part in a symposium of the German-Israeli Society of Ostfreisland (there is such a thing!) where German-Jewish (i.e., German-Israeli) relations were discussed under the motto "Forty Years Later–Genesis and Progression of a Strained Relationship." Quite a few participants had come to compare the Nazis' crimes against the Jews with the crimes of the Israelis against the Palestinians. Even those participants who didn't go quite so far declared themselves in some way responsible for the fate of the Palestinians. If the Germans had not persecuted the Jews, they opined, then the Jews today would not be persecuting the Palestinians. Through a chain of historical events, the Germans are responsible for the Palestinians, a fact used to justify telling the Israelis how they should treat the Palestinians. The larger reasoning was that this was, in the broadest sense, a German problem that just happened to take place in the Middle East. (In an essay on a similar theme, I struck upon the curious theory that the firmament of German history reached all the way to Palestinian soil.)

I agreed, adding the suggestion that we expand the German sphere of responsibility to include Togo, Zanzibar, and the Soviet Union. Togo was until 1914 a German colony, Zanzibar was traded with England in 1890 for Helgoland, and hadn't the Germans sent Lenin back to Russia in a sealed train car, in order that he might spread his revolutionary ideas there and weaken the Czarist regime? Would there be a Soviet Union today without Germany? Wouldn't Konigsberg still be German, Eastern Europe not communist, Berlin still undivided, and, for that matter, wouldn't the "news-magazine" of the Central German Television (ZDF) feel less obliged to feature East German dissidents?

This acute consciousness of responsibility seems like a drug that befuddles the drug dealer as well as the user. One of the most absurd examples of this effect comes from the pen of Wibke Bruhns, who left Israel after four years as a correspondent for *Der Stern* with a final column ("Farewell without Hope") and packed up to head for Washington. After repeatedly reassuring her readers that she is "bothered" by the situation in general, she complains as much about the lack of consideration among Israeli motorists as she does about the obstinacy of Jews and Arabs who are never prepared to compromise, then cites her shoe repairman and the man who sells her fish as representatives of public opinion. She finally ends her "farewell without hope" by concluding: "Nothing changes, I can change nothing, so it is only proper that I go. . . ."

Wibke Bruhns could have made it easy on herself. When *Der Stern* changed her assignment, she could have simply relocated from Jerusalem to Washington without having justified the move. But she preferred to emphasize her sense of responsibility. And since failing after you've tried in vain ranks higher on a moral currency scale than any degree of success—the hero, after all, has to experience his own tragedy before throwing in the towel—Wibke Bruhns didn't feel free to leave Israel until she had failed in her efforts to solve the Israeli-Arab conflict or, at the very least, to teach the Israelis better manners in traffic. "Nothing changes, I can change nothing, so it is only proper that I go. . . ."

"It's a deal, Wibke," one is tempted to yell after her, "we won't spite you for it! You gave it a shot!" In the last sentence, she tells us that she took with her "a rosemary bush, in a pot," and she is already in a Pan Am jet high above the clouds, course northwest, headed for new responsibilities. And who would dare, for complete lack of any sense of responsibility, to plop the question into the ice cubes clattering quietly in a glass of Chivas Regal: since when is it the job of correspondents to change the situations that they report on?

The most astonishing thing about such exercises is their Dr. Jekyll/Mr. Hyde effect. The worst prejudices are often substantiated by the very people one would least expect. Somewhere in the human mind there must be a "responsibility zone" that is coupled with the erectile tissue of our consciousness for responsibility, which, when stimulated, incites an uncontrollable reaction. At one time, an article like Wibke Bruhns's would have set me off completely and occasioned me to be as relentless as I was relishing of taking to task anything remotely reminiscent of German megalomania and pride. But I've since put several years' intensive training under my belt, and this has tended to put my relationship to Germany on a more relaxed footing. What is more, ever since I heard the phrase "I'm just doing my job" from an Israeli security officer in Jerusalem's El Al office, I know that "*typisch Deutsch*" ways of behaving aren't only to be found on German soil.

I don't get upset any more (at least not *as* upset), but I still register the facts: for example, the fact that the Fraternal Association of the "Honor-Standard Adolf Hitler" recognizes the Waffen-SS as a "public service organization," while at the same time they refuse to acknowledge the beliefs of a conscientious objector because the draft board failed to find in him "the special sensibility for the unconditional need to protect human life" just because he has a driver's license and drives a car. The fact is, the German Supreme Court ruled that the slogan "Turks out!" decorated with swastikas fails to constitute racial hate speech because, unlike the slogan "Jews out!" "generally recognized historical experiences are lacking"–it seems that the Turks, as the proverbial beer-hall wit might say, have yet to face the same fate the Jews have behind them. The fact is that the Chief Administrative Court, in a decision on the fate of a book in which the Nazis are relieved of all responsibility for the Second World War, decided to lift the ban on the book because "scientific opinion" on the events it depicts "is still in flux"–a ruling that really amounts to saying that it has not yet been determined that Hitler and the Nazis were responsible for the war.

All this doesn't quite drive me into the rage it used to, but it still does something to me. I have an ambivalent relationship to Germany, one shaped largely by the particular Germans I have had to deal with. After a seminar at the German-Israeli Society, full of very respectful people who are so unbearable precisely because they mean so well, I became convinced that the best that Germany has to offer are the crème pastries at Café Jansen in Cologne. But then I suddenly meet a young Christian theologian who thinks so soundly and undogmatically–in ways that I have never experienced on the German Left. I'm impressed, and I'm happy. Whether or not Chancellor Kohl goes to Bitburg is ultimately irrelevant, because I am certain that the distinction between the "decent" Wehrmacht and the "wicked" SS is so much idiotic hairsplitting. But Richard von Weizsäcker's May 8 speech could be a sign that Kohl, who cannot distinguish between Bitburg and Bergen-Belsen, is perhaps not representative of all of Germany, even when it might seem the case.

I was truly elated when I read in Israel that the first attempt to carry out a census in West Germany was thwarted by widespread resistance at the grassroots level. I thought: maybe "those Germans" (and not only the normal protest groupies who sign their name to every petition) have really learned, maybe they have really grasped that they must begin to mistrust the state and to say no when the situation demands it, not only to complain afterwards that they were deceived and seduced. This is why I find such actions, as miniscule and ultimately unsuccessful as they might be, extremely impressive and necessary. I am even impressed when, in Cologne, sixteen old trees scheduled to be bulldozed for a new parking garage are occupied and defended from the city's deforestation commandos, and even when animal rights activists rally against animal testing and maybe occasionally take apart a pharmaceutical lab. Every exercise of antiauthoritarianism, every refusal to submit to the wardens of the state and the powers that be is a good sign, a political and psychological step forward in a country where opposition borders on high treason and staying in line is considered a virtue. In this respect, some things have changed in Germany—for the better.

But such "antiauthoritarian" acts of resistance that I support not only at the level of sheer abstraction but also consider pragmatic are still problematic for me. These very same trees that I walked by for nine years on my way to school . . . I'm as unlikely to be concerned with their rescue as I am with the rights of animals to be free from cruelty, especially when compared to the same rights of people. The reason is quite simple. I ask myself where these same elderly people who fought so passionately for the trees in Cologne were and what action they took when my mother was hauled in a cattle car from one concentration camp to another. And about the young people who liberate the dogs and cats from their kennels in the research labs, I ask myself if they would act so resolutely if, today, Jews and Gypsies were being put in cages. With the older people, it is a rhetorical question that has already been answered by history. And with the young, I'm afraid the test results wouldn't come out much better than they did for the old. It could be that I am being unfair to many of these people. But my distrust is deep-seated, and it is substantiated again and again by a multitude of tiny observations and experiences made under the most peaceful conditions. When I read this sentence in a book valued as a standard reference for practicing animal rights activists—"The desire to inflict on others what one has oneself endured explains why it is not so seldom that one finds Jews among those who experiment on animals"–then I can be sure that even my cat and dog would agree that one can not be so sure of the dependability of German animal rights activists when it comes to the Jews.

Sometimes something happens that sets all of my ambivalences vibrating at once and shows me that my old attitudes are still there, just buried. Some time ago, the board of the German PEN Center decided to elect me to join their ranks. An old friend from Switzerland eventually shared the news with me, and I must admit that I felt honored. But things worked out quite differently. In a rather singular course of events, the board met again to withdraw my already successful election. The Frankfurt author Horst Krüger reported this story at a Haifa literature seminar: the leftist faction in PEN, represented by such seasoned class warriors and fine literary tastes as Margarete Mitscherlich and Gert von Paczensky, couldn't countenance my inclusion in the PEN Center because I had defamed the West German Left with the reproach of "covert anti-Semitism." Krüger, and with him a minority of the board, was horrified by the "conformism of the Left," but this minority was outnumbered and helpless.

When I learned about this "process," I felt–surprise, surprise–at once proud and insulted. The little opportunist deep in my soul (the one who wants to be recognized and loved even by the people he kicks in the ass) felt injured, unacknowledged, rejected, treated unfairly. At the same time, the Jewish child of the eastern ghetto thrust into Western civilization hovered a meter above the ground with pride and enthusiasm. What I wrote about left and bourgeois anti-Semitism, which has far exceeded "covert anti-Semitism," must have been right on the mark–it must have *really smarted*–if they had no other weapon against me but to deny me club membership. How self-assured and cool the advocates of free speech can be and how quickly they will resort to methods they would otherwise denounce as "repressive" and "reactionary" when it has to do with them personally. It is a comment not only on the sense of responsibility one has for one's own reputation but on the solitary sense of justice one has for one's comrades, or (Volks)-Genossen, who are forced to defend themselves against a provocation that, while it may be grounded, is simply beyond the pale.

And this sense of justice is a philosophy that crosses borders just as much as the sense of responsibility. Anyone who has exercised his sense of justice and injustice in trivial matters within his own organization will somehow not be able to remain silent when some injustice occurs out there in the great wide world. Although the firmament of German history reaches all the way to Palestinian soil, the sense of justice is a global Gulf Stream that begins in Husum and–sweeping by Schleswig-Holstein–travels all the way around the world until it ends on the coast of the Baltic Sea. And in between grows German rosemary—not in pots, but in hedges.

In a few weeks, I'll be traveling back to Cologne. On my shopping list are coffee and tea, Ovaltine and cocoa, candy and chocolate, moth balls and aluminum foil, mustard and radishes, White-Out and Scotch tape.

I am already looking forward to my trip to Karstadt.

*Translated by Kenneth McGill*

## TRANSLATOR'S NOTES

1. When the RAF's kidnapping of Hanns-Martin Schleyer failed in its aim to have three convicted RAF members (Andreas Baader, Jan-Carl Raspe, and Gudrun Ensslin) released from prison, the three committed suicide in Stammheim Prison in the fall of 1977.

2. Michael Kohlhaas is a character in the 1810 novella of the same name by Heinrich von Kleist. Kohlhaas's passionate sense of justice leads him to take the law in his own hands and ultimately to commit murder.

3. Broder is alluding to the late nineteenth- and early twentieth-century slogan, "Am deutschen Wesen soll die Welt genesen," rendered here as "the German nation shall be the world's salvation."

## OUR KAMPF

Once again the Germans have been betrayed by history, this time by particularly perfidious means. The Germans have managed to lose a war in which they did not even actively participate. Together with the defeated Iraqi army, the "noble souls" of the German peace movement have retreated from the battlefield.

How strange. While people everywhere else in the world breathed a sigh of relief, and while the Iraqi soldiers practically threw themselves in gratitude at the feet of the American GIs who'd captured them, a disquieting air of disappointment stole its way across Germany. What happened in the Gulf War was unfortunate, just not unfortunate enough. The long-awaited apocalypse never occurred, and despite Germany's aspirations and fears, the calamity never escalated to a Third World War. Even the global warming was kept at bay. And worse yet: the "oil carpet" from the Gulf stopped short of reaching Germany's Sylt Island resort.

Life has returned to normal. The soiled linens have been brought in from the balconies. The undistributed cards in memoriam of "our blessed Mother, the Earth" have landed in the recycling bin. The question "When Will We Be Wasted?" has vanished from the entrance gates of Humboldt University in Berlin. And suddenly the invitation to "Honk in Protest of the War" seems displaced in the empty lot. Indeed, the German peace movement had reached its most important objective in the war. During the scrimmage, the moral movement kept its hands clean from day one to the very end. In fact, many who had prepared for a longer war were denied the fruits of their labor. Those precisely 1,118 "male and female judges, prosecutors, defense attorneys, and legal advisors," for example, who had summoned an "End to the War *on* the Gulf" in full-page advertisements and called for the establishment of a "peace forum of legal advisors" were afforded the privilege, from one day to the next, of re-devoting themselves to the administration of criminal justice and civil rights. Even the tireless women of the Aktion Sheherezade were not able to put their plan into action. Their proposal, "World Jurisdiction Now!" was supposed to "listen to the opinions of each and every person in the world in this matter of life and death." Instead, two Sheherezade women traveled to New York to submit in person a petition with forty thousand signatures to UN Secretary General Perez de Cuellar.

But even this stack of signatures got "stuck somewhere along the way," and the secretary general sent his press agent to the women instead. The women told the spokesman that they wanted to see an "extraparliamentary World Security Council of Women" established that would have the right to "block all resolutions made by the World Security Council that are directed against human and women's rights or against the peaceful resolution of conflicts." According to one of the women's accounts delivered to a liberal faction in the Berlin House of Representatives upon her return from New York, the UN press agent had been "obviously impressed" by the proposal.

Actually, once the protagonists had exited the international arena and returned to their own moral sandboxes back home, the chapter on "The War on the Gulf and the German Peace Movement" could have been closed. There were only a few particularly noteworthy remarks made during the time between January 15 and February 28, 1991, that merit mentioning–a couple of historical footnotes to add to the story, so to speak. Allow us to let a few of our contemporaries speak for themselves–Gerhard Schröder, for example, an SPD (Social Democratic party) politician who was then the minister president of Lower Saxony.

Shortly after Saddam Hussein threatened to turn Israel into one enormous crematorium, Gerhard Schröder refused to endorse a solidarity statement with Israel because the statement's declaration did not encourage a cease-fire. On February 3, 1991, Gerhard Schröder had the opportunity to explain his stance on the SAT 1 television program "Talk im Turm" (Talk of the Tower). During the program, he claimed, "I vetoed it because I was being asked to both pledge my solidarity to Israel and support the war when I am not in favor of the war and cannot be in favor of the war. . . . I believe that whoever commits himself to the logic of war must be fully aware of what that entails. It means, namely, that if Saddam Hussein deploys lethal gas, the Western Alliance will discuss nuclear weapons in retaliation, and if you think this through, then you cannot exclude the possibility that nuclear weapons will in turn be deployed. This would result in a military scenario that would destroy the entire Middle East–Israel included–and ourselves and the fundamental security of young people everywhere. . . ."

Asked how he took the stance of the British, Gerhard Schröder stated, "I consider [England] a great country; and, since the pubs always closed at 11:30 P.M. when I was there, I watched a number of ridiculous TV movies that troubled me. Germans have been depicted as particularly bellicose war mongers, and I never found that a fair and accurate portrayal of the German people. But now–now the majority of Germans are saying 'We oppose the war,' and that isn't right either. You know, I am bothered by this British campaign, and I consider the reaction in Germany undignified–dog-eared and deferent to the opinions voiced over there. But those opinions are not justified. The British are not only negotiating this one conflict but a few other things as well, and well, it's about time that someone told them–and I am happy to be that someone–'hey, let's see you organize a rational, sociopolitically structured society and then we Europeans can discuss these issues on equal footing.'"

Okay, so the SPD hasn't yet gotten over the fact that they agreed to the war bonds of World War I and that retirement funds were sent to the Kaiser abroad. The party doesn't want to make another historical blunder. That's a feather in its cap. Yet, as a result, should the party go so far as to allow Gerhard Schröder to answer questions about moral and political affairs on its behalf? According to Schröder, one ought to be extremely cautious with Saddam Hussein so that he does not use lethal gas and the Americans do not deploy nuclear weapons–because this might result in radioactive fallout within his own political arena. That would be the real catastrophe. And if the pacifist Schröder, who does not want to take to the streets for Israel, does represent national interests, then he must be equally upset about the "dog-eared" and "deferent" reaction coming from Germany in response to the "British campaign" against Germany. What a stroke of luck that the Germans, instead of reacting submissively, can no longer launch a few V-2 shots to teach the British a lesson or two about respect, because–as behind the times as the British are–one cannot reason with them on "equal footing" now. Suddenly peace-loving, the German schoolmaster satisfies himself with having the sheer scientific know-how for producing and exporting B and C weapons and letting others do the dirty work for him. This is how the German social democracy deals not only with history but with every conflict from Baghdad to Buxtehude.

Another protagonist of the German's theatrical new desire for peace heightened by an old grudge against both the old and the new Allied Forces is Alice Schwarzer, the editor of the feminist magazine *Emma*. In an interview with Günter Jauch on Stern TV on January 23, 1991, she stated, among other things, that "generations of Arab peoples have been denigrated into slavery by their white masters and they have had it up to here [*gesturing with her hand up to her nose*]. They're at the end of their ropes. Later, there followed a period whereby both blocks, East and West, divvied up the entire region among themselves and the place is now, as we know, falling apart, just as the Third World is falling apart and the Arab world, too. . . . And the invasion of Kuwait is definitely problematic, but by no means outrageous. The country has only existed for about thirty years, and actually it was once Iraqi territory. However it came about, the conflict is there. But I am of the opinion that it would have been better had the Americans stayed at home. In the last decades (I have a good memory), they've blessed us with a myriad of conflicts in which they felt, for whatever reason, they had to meddle. This resulted in millions of casualties on both sides. . . ."

And in response to the question of Iraqi missile attacks on Israel, Alice Schwarzer responded: "They are very dramatic. They are in and of themselves very dramatic. I mean endangered and dead people–that's always a tragedy. They were also related to us Germans, because the fact that Israel exists, and thank God it exists, has much to do with the Holocaust and fascism–which is particularly painful. However, I believe the safest thing for Israel in the long run is to maintain a peaceful coexistence with its neighbors. Anything else would deter Israel from making progress. . . ."

Whoever is familiar with the eloquence with which our *Emma* editor customarily makes her appearance can only puzzle over the awkward off-guardedness throughout her response. If we leave her embarrassed interjections aside, only one assertion remains: the missile attacks on Israel were "for us Germans particularly painful." Once again, the Jews got the better end of the bargain. Whereas they only had to deal with SCUD missiles whipping past their ears, "for us Germans" the whole Holocaust resurfaced overnight.

Can we conclude that our protagonist struggles with a certain ill-ease when it comes to Israel and the Jews, yet can address other questions cavalierly? In the latter, the Third World doesn't fall apart. The invasion of Kuwait, we learn, was "definitely problematic, but by no means outrageous." Okay, so it is about like sexually assaulting a woman who resists the advances of a courtier but is taken by force anyway. Problematic, but not at all outrageous. That Kuwait has existed as a nation for "only about thirty years" is an argument of similar charm. For one, the Federal Republic of Germany as a country is only ten years older, and secondly, a number of countries are even younger than that. The Americans, she maintains, would be better off at home. Furthermore, in the context of her argument, namely her reference to the "myriad of conflicts" and the "millions of casualties," you could infer that she not only refers to the latest intervention but to those that lay forty-five years back as well. In that case, Alice Schwarzer would not be editing *Emma* but a Nazi magazine for the Professional Association of Aryan Women at best, and, in the final analysis, when it comes down to details like judging U.S. imperialism, the difference between them would not be all that great. The thought of where she would be today and what she might be doing if the Americans had stayed home back then wouldn't seem to tarnish her worldview, in spite of her great memory. Alice Schwarzer could lean back satisfied and say with ease, "I'm really glad that the Americans don't have any reason to come to *our* aid."

In the March edition of *Emma*, Alice Schwarzer lays it on one more time. "Since the 17th of January we find ourselves in a Third World War," she exclaims and can't resist drawing an analogy to the Second World War: "In the first evening alone, more bombs fell on Baghdad than on Dresden during the entire duration of World War II." By the time the article was published, the "Third World War" was already over, but in the event that a fourth should break out anytime soon, Alice Schwarzer provides us with an insight into who was actually responsible for the entire drama: the Jews and their affiliates in the White House. "For a long time now, Israel has had an extralegal government that fueled the flame of hatred against the Arabs. Should this one day pose a threat to Israel's existence—and that would be terrible—then above all Falk, Shamir, Bush, and Schwarzkopf would be to thank. And Israel is not only the refuge and home of the Jews, rather Israel was and is a Western outpost to the Arab World. As an outpost, Israel will, by way of its pro-Semite pretense, escalate its armament until it is in possession of the nuclear bomb."

Whichever accusations one wishes to make, Frau Doktor Alice Schwarzer is certainly not a "pro-Semite," rather something of a bigot. On the one hand, she announces the beginning of the "Third World War." On the other hand, she asserts that Israel's existence is not immediately threatened but will be in the future—as a result of its own misdeeds.

This new German innocence, the Left's variation of the blessing of late birth, also brought Hans Christian Ströbele to make a statement that he still to this day considers accurate, only poorly formulated: "The Iraqi missile attacks on

Israel are the logical, indeed the inevitable, consequence of Israeli politics." Only a few days before making this statement, he said—just as casually—in a telephone conversation with the Green party's local representative from Tübingen, Christian Vogt-Moykopf, "If I could prevent an escalation of the war with the death of a million Jews, I would accept that as the price of doing business." The occasion for that conversation and assertion was a letter that several Baden-Württemburg representatives of the Green party, including Vogt-Moykopf, wrote to the Israeli ambassador in Bonn. In the letter, they expressed approval toward the delivery of Patriot missiles to Israel. "After the public disclosure of the letter, Ströbele called me in parliament. He said I was always such a 'rational person' and didn't understand why I would promote the delivery of Patriots and, in certain cases, the deployment of troops 'to that country.' ... Any delivery of weapons to Israel would result in an 'escalation of the war and conflict in the Middle East in general....' I inquired further as to whether or not he cared about the lives of perhaps thousands of people. He replied in these exact words. 'If I could prevent an escalation of the war with the death of a million Jews, I would accept that as the price of doing business.'"

After this statement was publicized, Vogt-Moykopft received a request from Ströbele's lawyer "to refrain in the future from claiming that Mr. Ströbele stated...." The attorney's letter maintained, among other things, that "Mr. Ströbele never made such an assertion. Furthermore, the details of a confidential conversation between the two of you were publicized.... Mr. Ströbele did not authorize the public disclosure of what allegedly took place in the course of this confidential conversation."

Are we dealing here with the alleged details of a confidential conversation or an alleged conversation with confidential details? If we understand correctly the implications of the letter written by Ströbele's lawyer, we can interpret it bearing this in mind: Ströbele held a discussion behind closed doors and assumed that his partner would keep its contents to himself. "The confidentiality guaranteed by attorneys to their clients does not apply when anti-Semitic conduct is at hand," said Christian Vogt-Moykopf, "and especially not when politicians are involved who otherwise are so eager to seek publicity."

The question of whether Ströbele stated his opinion in confidence or by accident or—like Kohl, Jenninger, Fellner, and others before him—whether his remark didn't reflect his own opinion is one that will have to be left to later inquiries. However, it is certain that he revealed the stance of a fraction of the Green party platform. After resigning in the interests of the party, statements were not only issued from the famous German Communist party artist Degenhardt, with a letter to the editor of the *taz* newspaper ("Dear Ströbele, I extend my sincere congratulations .."); declarations of solidarity also came from less renowned friends of peace who were touched by Ströbele's remarks. He was the "first prominent politician from the Green party, in fact, the whole Federal Republic, who dared to state a few frank facts about Israeli politics that challenged the cowardly black-and-white political viewpoints expressed until now," wrote a *taz* reader. "Ströbele was totally right in that part about the important consequences," seconded another. "Ströbele is absolutely right!" "Without the Israeli political agenda of the past years there probably never would have been an Iraqi attack," affirmed a third.

Many letters to the editor of the ostensibly liberal *taz* read like columns of the Nazi *Nationalzeitung.* And many were exact replicas of the type that occasioned Adorno and Horkheimer to conclude that Germany's problem was not the Nazis but their opponents. "The hypocritical actions of Joschka Fischer, various fractions within the so-called peace movement, and others just cannot be tolerated any longer. When will we finally rid ourselves of a past that doesn't allow us to pass judgment? The protest movements alone in Germany show that 'we Germans' learned something from the past. But, nevertheless, that troubles the war buddies Shamir and Bush."

And so the right wing's conviction that finally Germany must step out from under the "shadow of Auschwitz" has been tailored to fit the agenda of the Left. Whereas in the past the *parole* "The Jews are our misfortune!" was the norm, the peace movement agreed this time upon the motto: "The Jews are responsible for their own misfortune!"

That Saddam Hussein announced his intentions to destroy Israel a long time ago was either ignored or bagatelled. "We just didn't have time to address the threat to Israel," explained Brigitte Erler on the eve of a large peace demonstration in Bonn. As the first Iraqi missiles struck Tel Aviv, the protest calls had already gone to the press. . . . And if earlier every respectable German took a Jew into hiding, even if only temporarily, then almost every German friend of peace had a Jewish or Israeli friend with whom he shared his commiserate understanding of the situation in an open letter. "In the long run, it is not the missiles that immediately threaten Israel's right to live in peace. Rather, it is the unresolved Palestinian conflict and the hostility on the part of its Arab neighbors," proclaimed one West German friend of peace in *Die Zeit* to an Israeli woman, who must have found great comfort in this noble and clever remark as she and her children wore gas masks in a sealed room while waiting for the next missile attack and worrying to death about their future together.

And where the real danger could not be denied even by the best intentions, then at least the roles of cause and effect had to be distorted and reversed. "Wasn't Israel only endangered as a consequence of U.S. military intervention in the Iraqi occupation of Kuwait?" Andreas Buro asked participants at the peace demonstration in Bonn. It was, of course, a rhetorical question, as her subsequent statement illustrates: "Since then, SCUD missiles have been falling, and a fear of lethal gas has spread." By the same logic, one could also justify taking hostages in a bank robbery by saying that only after the police intervened were the hostages really in danger. Before then, everything was relatively harmless. This, then, became the logical and almost inevitable consequence of that attitude whenever the question was raised as to the price of peace and who should pay it. "Not even the unconscionable aggression of Hussein, not even his willingness to perpetuate genocide against Israel in particular justifies a war," said the state superintendent of the Lippian church, Ako Haarbeck.

And his East German comrade, the bishop of Berlin-Brandenburg, Gottfried Forck, made clear with an example from everyday life just how one could deal with Suddam Hussein. "This lunatic stands on the roof of a house with a bomb in his hand that could kill not only himself, but a multitude of innocent bystanders as well. My objective, then, would be to convince him with reasonable and persuasive words to come down so that I could disarm him." In addition, Bishop Forck recommended another method of debilitating the Iraqi dictator: "The people of Iraq must be encouraged by us to position themselves in defense against this terrorist regime. . . . I am reminded of our resistance against the SED regime in the GDR. As we took to the streets, no one thought that such a rapid dissolution of the system was possible. In the end, we were all surprised and bewildered by our own success. This victory is a sign for me that, in practice, one ought to resort more often to nonviolence."

Bishop Forck was not the only one who, under the impression of Iraqi aggression, began to think about the advantages of nonviolent resistance. At the occasion, the political scientist Ekkehart Krippendorff saw in this an opportunity to take recourse to the writings of Mahatma Gandhi and Martin Buber in order to illustrate how the Third Reich could have been torn from its hinges—namely, through passive resistance by the Jews against the Nazis. "Just imagine the following scenario: not one German Jew follows the discriminating regulations of the German authorities (the Star of David, the segregated park benches, restricted shopping hours, etc.)—would they, up against hundreds of thousands, have been able to prevail? Just imagine if not a single German Jew followed the order to gather at the deportation sites—a few dozen, a few hundred, maybe even a hundred thousand (passive resistance!)—the German police may have been able to drive so many from their homes and load them onto the trucks; but hundreds of thousands? . . . Or just imagine that colonies of hundreds, thousands just sat clean down on their way to the commercial train stations—a 'sit-in strike' is what we call that today—would the police, the SA, the Wehrmacht, and the SS have risked beating so many people regardless of their age and gender before the eyes of every German, and would they have loaded body after permissive but powerful body into the freight trains? . . . It is at least legitimate to speculate as to whether or not the regime would have self-destructed in the wake of such massive passive resistance."

The speculation is legitimate, as is the answer: those who ask such questions understand just enough about the nature of totalitarian regimes to serve as a professor at the Otto Suhr Institute. What remains is the bizarre accusation that the NS regime didn't collapse because the Jews never organized a sit-in strike at the loading docks.

The ink spilled over this meganonsense was not yet dry when Krippendorff stepped up to the next round of academic sack races. In response to an article in which I recommended keeping the war at bay by having the Pope migrate to Baghdad and sending a high-caliber German delegation to Tel Aviv, he offered yet another scenario: "Just imagine if Israel would withdraw unconditionally today from the occupied territories, accept the corresponding UN resolutions, and immediately grant the Palestinians the right to elect their own representatives and create a sovereign Palestinian state: that would be the most difficult and most decisive long-term defeat for Saddam Hussein." And with that, he had issued his second accusation. Not only did the Jews neglect to dismantle the Third Reich through passive resistance, they brought the war against Saddam Hussein upon themselves because of their ridiculous refusal to "withdraw unconditionally today from the occupied territories." Even before Ströbele cried out "it's your own fault," the impact of Iraqi missiles in Israeli cities and the respective celebration of the Palestinians was, according to Krippendorff, "the storm that the politics of the state of Israel gave wind to."

With this, Professor Krippendorff considers himself a friend of Israel, much like Walter Jens believes he is an ally of the Jews. Jens is fond of defending this by quoting Albert Einstein, Yeshayahu Leibowitz, Martin Buber, and Gustav Landauer. In his own words: "especially those [of us] allies of the Jewish people, above all those who are also prepared to contemplate the ideas of the novelist Yoram Kaniuk, who once said that the Germans always loved only the victims and ignored the brave activists among the Jews . . . especially we, I wanted to say, who for years have been charged with crude philo-Semitism by militant right-wingers, should take care, I think, to issue an unrelenting declaration of solidarity that would to the very end stand by those who rightfully refrain from newly manifesting their aversion to the crimes of the RAF."

Is there anyone in the Federal Republic, including the five new states, who can explain to us just what Professor Walter Jens means by this? That he does not want to be *accused* of crude philo-Semitism, especially not from the militant right wing, which is otherwise his greatest concern? Does he mean that those who manifest their aversion to the crimes of the RAF, or those who refrain from such manifestations, should remain silent about Israel's affairs? Does Walter Jens refer to the Red Army Faction or the Royal Air Force? I really don't know. I know only one thing: with friends like this, you no longer need fear your enemies.

As it stands, I prefer those who speak their minds and do not pretend to be friends of the Jewish people. Like the representative Vera Wollenberger (Bündnis 90/Green Party Coalition), for example, who, after her return from a fact-finding mission to Syria and Jordan, declared that delivering arms to Israel would be "extremely dangerous because it would further exacerbate the atmosphere in the Arab world." Here I'd like to thank representative Wollenberger for her contribution to the political statements made on Ash Wednesday, because she referred to a causal relationship in simple and unequivocal terms: the better Israel's survival chances, the worse the atmosphere in the Arab world. With this remark, it was immediately clear to even the last friend of peace in Radebeul how one could cure the Arabs of their resentment.

The same sentiment, though phrased differently, was expressed by the honorary chairman of the PDS (Party of Democratic Socialists), Hans Modrow, who asserted that "the only real protection for Israel could be ensured by not delivering any arms whatsoever." This statement was made by the PDS/SED functionary who during his term under the NVA (National People's Army) of the GDR was responsible for instructing friends of the Iraqi army in the proper handling of chemical weapons.

What does this go to show? In ordinary human interactions, an intentional failure to offer humanitarian assistance could be seen as aiding and abetting a crime. Whoever neglects to come to the aid of a neighbor in need and instead gives him a lecture on brotherly love, whoever initiates a debate with a drowning man on whether or not to throw him a line seeing as how he put himself in the boat he's in by failing to have learned to swim, whoever embarks on such a course of action shall at the very least refrain from assuming the guise of a well-meaning friend. At some point, even a hypocrite must be held up to shame. Whoever behaves this way must also ask whether or not he really does want to watch the inevitable misfortune occur as a result of his chosen stance.

After the first Iraqi missiles had landed in Israel, Joschka Fischer claimed that the "implications" of the missile attacks against Tel Aviv did "not hit home as they should have." The protest "Hands off Israel!" was supposed to have the same connotation as "Stop the War! Now!" Here Joschka Fischer was gravely mistaken. The Iraqi assault against Israel hit home with the brothers of the peace movement just as it was supposed to. That the offensive did not provoke indignation and exasperation, as Fischer may have liked, has one simple reason. The likely destruction of Israel was accepted by all as the logical and almost inevitable (in other words, *deserved*) consequence of Israel's political policy. It was this conviction that supplied Saddam Hussein with a sympathy bonus point he could not have achieved through his clamorous anti-imperialist campaign alone.

Just to make my point clear: I do not intend to claim that a majority of Germans would like to see Israel destroyed; rather, I think that quantitatively and qualitatively a substantially great portion of the peace movement was motivated by an unconscious, albeit exceedingly intense desire to believe that Saddam Hussein wanted to cash in on a historical opportunity to polish off the job the Nazis could not finish. Then, finally, the Germans would be able to curb an inhibition that, "in the wake of German history," keeps us from saying exactly what we'd like to say, but cannot. "We," meaning the good Germans, would finally be "relieved of the burdens of a historical past that does not warrant us the liberty of free expression." In other words, with the second Final Solution to the Jewish Question in Palestine, the past could finally disappear in history's final curtain call. And by a stroke of luck, sufficient evidence would be supplied to prove that no one can live in peace with the Jews, not even the Arabs who are Semites by rite of birth.

Krippendorff would call such a deliberate consideration a "scenario." I find it the logical, almost inevitable consequence of the recriminations that surfaced during the Six Week War. One ought to mull this over for a while. At the same time that Saddam Hussein's pledge to annihilate Israel was not taken seriously, even minimized, people were painting a scenario of a "Third World War" that would cost us "several million victims" (Vera Wollenberger). German youth who lingered about with the forewarnings "When Will We Be Wasted?" and "Today It Was the Gulf–and Tomorrow?" while distributing memorials for "Our beloved Mother, the Earth" simultaneously proclaimed that Israel shouldn't put up such a fuss over a few missiles and ought to withdraw instead from the occupied territories. Even if they might be seen objectively as confused souls, they knew exactly what they were doing. If one accused them of nurturing their pacifism on the backs of a third party, then they would have replied that they had taken their lesson from German history. The use of force should never again be used as a vehicle for political change. They seem to me like anxious and rehabilitated violent criminals who watch with utter composure as a mugger takes a passerby to the cleaners without interceding because they have renounced the use of force on moral grounds and want to avoid a relapse at all costs. That the peace movement was unmoved by the massacres carried out by Iraqi troops against Shiites and Kurds and was just as silent in the wake of the Iraqi invasion of Kuwait that directly preceded the war could have disturbed only those who put their faith in representatives who claimed that they were not motivated by anti-American sentiments.

On April 13, 1991, the *Frankfurter Rundschau* published a critical response from Dr. Andreas Buro to an article written by the newspaper's editor, Reifenrath. Reifenrath, the speaker of the Committee on Fundamental Human Rights in Bonn-Beuel, attempted to find an answer to a question that had been circulating at the time: Why doesn't the peace movement take to the streets en masse to protest the mass murder of Kurds? In Buro's opinion, this could not be expected of the peace movement, because "what kind of superhumans did we want these demonstrators to be when they constantly . . . should be out in the streets, but, at the same time, have to earn a living and still want to live well and have the same kind of pastimes that every other man and woman has?" After all, "at any given time there are at least ten to twenty wars going on in the world," and "people are tortured incessantly in any number of countries. I mean, human rights are abused left and right."

He sure is right about that. Even the most devoted peace fighters are breadwinners, too. It simply wouldn't be fair to expect them to miss their belly-dancing lessons and Ikebana sessions continuously because of some war. If we were kind, we would grant them the relief and replenished strength their pastimes afford. Then the next time we're up against U.S. imperialism or a Zionist offensive campaign, they'll be fit to join in on the fun.

*Translated by Andrea Scott*

7

## JUST BETWEEN GERMANS

If you were to attempt to demonstrate to a visitor from another planet what Germany is today—the state of this country in the first third of the nineties in the twentieth century—you would have to take the guest by the hand and lead him to the House at Checkpoint Charlie in Berlin. It is a private museum where the history of the Berlin Wall is documented and an assortment of curiosities is on exhibit, like a Mini-Cooper and a hang glider used by GDR citizens in successful escapes across the German-German border.

German-German encounters of a very special kind take place at irregular intervals at the House at Checkpoint Charlie—so-called perpetrator-victim talks, where former collaborators with "State Security" (the Stasi) come together with their former "clients," former opponents of the system who were observed, spied on, and if need be driven to the brink of emotional collapse by the Stasi. It is a spectral ritual of remarkable entertainment value. The perpetrators and the victims sit around a large table and explain to each other how it was "back then," when the "informal collaborator" X spied on his friend Z at the behest of his supervising officer Y, unbeknownst to Z, of course, even if he had some inkling that he was under surveillance by the Stasi.

These conversations have to be imagined as a sort of group-dynamic and group-therapeutic event. Six or seven exposed ex-Stasi collaborators, professional as well as informal, sit on a stage and "come clean." Some more readily than others. Some speak freely and without holding back, while from others every sentence must be laboriously extracted. Seventy or eighty spectators sit in the hall, many of whom have had some degree of involvement with the Stasi and now want to know why they were placed under surveillance and what on earth the Stasi people were thinking about their own activities. Every now and then someone loses control.

"So once again, it's nobody's fault!" a man in the hall yells suddenly. "Which one of you put me in the can—I did three years for saying that the GDR was going downhill—who do I have to thank for that?" The Stasi people on stage look around unmoved. None of them feels as though he has anything to do with this.

Despite the occasional outburst from Stasi victims, the Perpetrator-Victim Talks are an altogether friendly sort of gathering. Next to the large table where the ex-Stasi are seated, someone has set up a smaller table with two large platters of sandwiches, a cheesecake, and a big thermos of coffee. Every few minutes, one of the spectators trudges forward from the audience to get a sandwich or a cup of coffee and some cake, then returns to his seat. It must have been almost as back then, when the IMs[1] chatted up the objects of their prying secret-service curiosity or their supervising officers. And yet, you learn some very interesting things.

There's an ex-pastor here who was signed on as an IM. He was an oppositionist and adversary of the system, and as such he was contacted one day by a Stasi officer. "If you want to change the conditions in the GDR, why not do it in friendly cooperation with us? There's no point in standing against us." That seemed clear enough to him.

There's also a full-timer, who resigned the service just before the Wende and now praises the "peaceful revolution." "There's never been anything like it in any country—a revolution where not a single windowpane was broken."

These are no miscreants sitting here together, dark figures with demonic auras, just scores of ordinary people like you and me: this one's overweight, that one's got a beard like Popeye the Sailor, another would do well to wash his hair once in a while. If you were going to stage a play about the "banality of evil," you'd have to cast it with these people.

Werner Fischer, an accomplished civil-rights activist in the former GDR, moderates the meeting. He wants to please everyone. "There isn't just the one-dimensional IM on this side, and the noble oppositionist on the other—there's a whole personal biography locked up in each of them," he says in his opening statement. One should consider the topic "with composure" and "leave the hysteria behind." Then the participants are introduced. Here sits a well-known dissident, who was himself active for a short time in the Stasi as a young FDJ secretary[2] and came clean with it before he could be outed. There sit three "informal collaborators" who were active in opposition groups, among them a youth pastor from Jena; there is a professional Stasi agent, who carried out systematic "undermining work"; there a GDR writer who was terrorized, arrested, and tortured by the Stasi. If it went according to the laws of nature they would have to get up and beat on each other; yet since only German history is getting "worked over" here, the victims ask the perpetrators for an explanation. Here it isn't always clear to what extent the perpetrators were also victims and vice-versa—a classic German dilemma.

Lothar P., for instance, a man of indeterminate age in an inconspicuous gray suit, was recruited by the Stasi at eighteen. He had just completed his Abitur, and the offer to work for the Stasi came at an opportune time, "out of lust for adventure, somehow to get out of this boring GDR." He tells his story incoherently, with time lapses that are difficult to follow. This much is clear: at some point the Stasi let him go and then signed him on again in 1985 to inform on the "Peace and Human Rights" initiative. "It was the mistake of my life," says Lothar P., who was allowed to study philosophy in the GDR and worked on "developmental planning" at the Academy of the Sciences. The Stasi, the way he sees it today, was "a criminal organization, like the NSDAP and the RAF." After the public round of talks, in an interview with a journalist, Lothar P. elaborates: "It isn't about excluding ex-Stasi people from society forever, you can't let them turn into welfare cases. That makes no sense for the taxpayers either." As to what he does professionally, Lothar P. is not willing to be very specific. He has "prospects for self-employment."

Walter Templin, one of the more prominent GDR dissidents, sits next to Lothar P. Lothar P. and Templin were friends, which is why P. turns to Templin while speaking and occasionally calls him "Wölfchen." Templin looks straight ahead and ignores this conciliatory gesture. P. was assigned to Templin; he was supposed to report back to the Stasi on the effects their "undermining tactics" were having on the civil-rights activist. There was one operation that lasted over three months, from January to April 1986. Every day ten to twenty people would show up at the Templins' to deliver things that they had "ordered": furniture, appliances, ornamental fish; once it was an order of condoms big enough for an army unit. Workers came from far and wide to repair the Templins' house. What sounds like a comedy was pure terror. The operation ended after Lothar P. reported to the Stasi that Templin would survive but that his wife and children might be emotionally shattered by it. Lothar P. holds to his credit that the Stasi campaign against Templin was called off because of his report. He seems to be waiting for a word of thanks from Templin. But Templin is not grateful. He points out that the same report could have inspired the Stasi to continue the campaign until he had capitulated in order to spare his family.

Lothar P. received small paybacks for his work—fifty marks here, a hundred marks there. But money wasn't important to him. Recently he has thought intensively about why he collaborated. "If you're not a political criminal, does that mean the condition for going along is that you don't worry about what they're using the reports for?" How can you not think about it, though, when you're spying on friends and betraying them to the state? "We all lived under the assumption the that GDR would always be there. And the main thing was that somebody told the political leadership the truth about what people were thinking. Only the Stasi could do that. So the Stasi had to be kept informed. Otherwise, you couldn't talk to anybody about what was really going on."

Two seats over sits Konstantin S., a former youth pastor from Jena. Since then, Konstantin has achieved a small measure of fame as an IM. There's even been a film made about him, in which he willingly reenacts scenes from his life as a Stasi informant. He was active in the Jungen Gemeinde in Jena, an evangelistic youth group that opposed the system. And everything that happened in the group was immediately laid on the table for the Stasi—by way of Konstantin S., who now says, "I'm angry with myself!" and asks himself, "what were you thinking?" The group got together, talked, and drank, and while all the others went home to sleep, "I still had to sit myself down and write a report." Konstantin S. functioned without a second thought, without a guilty conscience, without considering the consequences: "Every IM did something, but none of them did anything substantial, so everyone could say: they can't really do anything with the information I'm giving them."

Between the two IMs, Lothar P. and Konstantin S., sits a full-time ex-Stasi-man by the name of Schachtschneider, a real secret-agent pro. He "supervised" a whole series of IMs. His assignment was to see to it that doctors who wanted to leave the GDR abandoned their plans and stayed in the republic. Schachtschneider would rather not go into the methods employed to these ends. "There was a whole range of measures, the Ministry of State Security was willing to go to very great lengths. . . ."

Someone in the audience wants to know if Schachtschneider *thought about* Gestapo methods. He obviously misunderstands the question and says, "They weren't our daily tools. Openly terrorist methods, such as during fascism, weren't feasible in the GDR." When a woman in the hall yells, "Not true, it wasn't like that!" the moderator intervenes. This wasn't about hate, wasn't about revenge; everything must be brought into the open in detail, "only then is reconciliation possible."

The Ministry of State Security, Schachtschneider continues, was "to blame"; as for individuals, it would be hard to see where they fit into the whole. "Explain *your* position!" yells someone in the hall, to which Schachtschneider responds, "I had to make sure that physicians didn't leave the GDR." "Did you undermine people?" someone interjects. Schachtschneider gets a little more concrete: "I prevented people from leaving the GDR—by every means available. . . ." "What did you do?" the person who interrupted wants to know. Lothar P. intervenes and yells back, "Everybody knows what was done!" The person in the audience asks no further questions.

The more reserved the Stasi people are in the presentation of their activities, the more they—unwittingly—create an understanding of a totalitarian system. Schachtschneider manages to sum up the reality of the GDR in one sentence: "Every GDR citizen was afraid of the Stasi; many attempted to step out of harm's way by trying to participate in that power."

The Stasi was not only a terror apparatus, it was also a participatory model that provided myriad opportunities to grab a little part of the state's omnipotence. Every minor IM could conceive of himself as a part of the greater whole, at once significant and protected. For Thomas G., who never had anything to do with the FDJ, drifted long-haired through the GDR, and considered himself an "outsider," the Stasi was "a kind of surrogate parent; they were people who took care of others." He had a "personal relationship" with his contact officer, and beyond that, it was important to him "to change something through realistic reports. . . ."

Sometime in the course of the talks, the writer Siegmar Faust says he's amazed that there's "no great difference between the IMs and those under surveillance." In fact, the IMs present also see themselves as oppositionists who wanted to at least change, if not subvert, the system from within. And the full-time Stasi people like Schachtschneider don't want to be seen as the villains that they were. They admit that they did evil—even if in firm belief in good.

"What stands before us all is a process of mastering our past," the host says at the end of the panel, releasing the audience to go home with the feeling that the relevant issues have not yet been laid on the table.

*Translated by Hunter Bivens*

## TRANSLATOR'S NOTES

1. Informelle Mitarbeiter, or informal collaborator, was the term used by the Stasi to describe people who worked for the Stasi without formally being on the payroll of the Ministry of State Security.

2. Freie Deutsche Jugend, or the Free German Youth, was the name of the East German youth group.

8

# A BEAUTIFUL REVOLUTION

Slowly but surely a suspicion is rising from the sunken abyss of the GDR: maybe the Stasi wasn't what it was held to be in the West. Maybe it wasn't a repressive state apparatus terrorizing the people, but rather a kind of VEB[1] "Social Safety Net" covering the country like a blanket, catching the reprobates and resocializing them, and also functioning like a trampoline, which means bouncing those who deserved it into higher positions.

"It is one of the most grotesque mistakes of the West German intelligentsia that they ignored the effects of the Mielke apparatus for decades,"[2] writes Carl Corino, a West German expert on conditions in the "Zone."[3] By this he means "the total saturation of everyday life in the GDR."

And Rolf Schneider, who also comes from "over there," says, "this institution, in possession of information about every past and pending event in the country, equipped with the latest technology and an army of highly paid assistants, failed at the very endeavor that it was created to prevent or avert. . . . the epochal comedy is unparalleled, but no one wants to admit it."

Rolf Schneider doesn't notice that he has drawn false conclusions from an accurate analysis. Why should the Stasi, in possession of information about every past and pending event in the country, equipped with the latest technology and an army of highly paid assistants, have failed? The opposite was the case: The Stasi perfected its work with the so-called Wende. The "peaceful revolution" was its magnum opus; it saved the best for last.

That sounds somewhat absurd, like a Perry Rhodan story in Saxon dialect. Yet, if one looks at the situation without preconceived notions and places the known facts in relation to each other, the suspicion becomes more plausible. If what Markus Wolf and Alexander Schalk-Golodkowski have said has any credibility, the Stasi knew well in advance about the collapse of the GDR; it was, as Rolf Schneider says, in possession of information about *all* events in the country, past and pending. It was clear to the Stasi people they had to do something to secure, if not their privileges, then at least their material survival on the highest possible level; in other words, not in a West German holding tank for GDR refugees. A simple dissolution of the moribund state apparatus through a declaration of bankruptcy was as unworkable as a direct handover to the Federal Republic. Therefore a mass movement had to be created that would put pressure on politicians in the GDR as well as the FRG to take action. The liquidation of the GDR had to be fully legal and carried out by completely "peaceful means."

It comes across like Joe Millerism pulled on history that the first free elections to the East German Parliament, the Volkskammer, were organized to create a legislative body with only one task: to abolish itself. Nothing like this has ever happened in the history of parliamentary democracy; states have certainly gone under, but none in so orderly a fashion as the GDR. It is equally unique that the top positions in the revolutionary movement were occupied by security apparatus collaborators, whose actual task was the prevention of revolutionary change: de Maizière in the CDU, Ibrahim Böhme in the SPD, Wolfgang Schnur in the Demokratischer Aufbruch, to name only the most prominent. Is it then thinkable that they acted on their own initiative against the Big Brother who called them to duty and guided their steps?

If the Stasi knew everything, if it was informed about everything in advance, if no action was possible against it, then it also orchestrated the Wende. Which is certainly not to say that every demonstrator was out on assignment for the Stasi. That wasn't necessary anyway. It was enough that each demonstrator was appropriately instrumentalized.

In the meantime, the extent to which the Stasi infiltrated the churches, the underground cultural scene, and the peace movement has become apparent.

If Mielke's boys managed to put an agent ("Donald") in Vera Wollenberger's bed,[4] should it then be any coincidence that the former Stasi General Markus Wolf attempted to place himself at the head of the "peaceful revolution"? On November 4, 1989, as a million people gathered on Alexanderplatz, he went for a walk through the city with his dog Nikita, and as he strolled by the "Alex," he thought: "Since I'm here, I might as well say something too." And was it also then coincidence that wherever an outraged mob made plans to storm a Stasi office, speakers of the "movement" were always immediately in place to reestablish peace and order? And were there anywhere acts of retaliation against exposed Stasi charges? On the contrary, when the newspaper *die andere* began publishing lists of official Stasi collaboraters over the course of several issues, half of the ex-GDR shook with indignation at this "denunciation." And was anyone harmed through this revolution? There weren't even any windowpanes broken.

The higher the rank, the better the survival chances for Stasi officers. Entire departments were discreetly swallowed up by the free market. Markus Wolf, had he not been faced with criminal proceedings, would have applied for his takeover by the official service of the Federal Republic. He could have cited a historical parallel for this. Nazi officials were also taken on, or rather pensioned off, commensurate with their previous salaries. An administrative court in Berlin has ruled that previous Stasi activity does not fundamentally preclude official service to the Federal Republic.

Those who find it difficult to accept that the "peaceful revolution" was a show put on by the Stasi in their efforts to protect themselves not only lack political imagination, they're still stuck in a James Bond and Dr. No mentality. A modern secret service thinks about nothing but itself to the very end. It facilitates a "corporate identity," and it is ready to sacrifice the system it serves to its own interests. No one knew better than the Stasi how pointless holding on to the GDR would be. And no one was in a better position to determine the manner and time of the leave-taking.

What remains? The peaceful revolution in the GDR was a sociopolitical measure sponsored from above. It was carried out by the type of revolutionary already mocked in Erich Mühsam's song about the "revolutionary wannabe." Lamp cleaner by trade, he was highly concerned, lest through the revolution his lanterns might come to some harm.

That's the beauty of German revolutions: you know the outcome in advance.

*Translated by Hunter Bivens*

## TRANSLATOR'S NOTES

1. Volkseigener Betrieb, or People's Own Enterprise, was the usual designation for East German industrial and commercial concerns

2. Erich Mielke was the minister of state security of the GDR from 1957 until the collapse of SED rule in 1989.

3. It was often customary in the Federal Republic to refer to the GDR as the Soviet Zone for propaganda purposes.

4. Vera Wollenberger was a prominent civil-rights activist, and Member of Parliament after 1989, in the GDR.

9

## A HOPELESS ENLIGHTENMENT

My Viennese friend Peter, who shares my deep love of Habsurg dirt, Mickey Mouse, and Countess Marizza, thinks *Schindler's List* is a "bad film," a "well-made, but very bad film." What counts against it, says Peter, is above all "the fact that it was strategically marketed from the first day of shooting" and that all Spielberg wanted was to "finally secure his recognition as a director," to claim the Oscars he didn't get for *Indiana Jones* or *Jaws*. Peter's objections to Spielberg's movie can be summed up in one word: "Hollywood."

My Viennese friend Peter isn't the only one who thinks this way. Many intellectuals, who are otherwise always complaining about people's lack of interest in history in general and in "mastering the past" in particular, have a difficult time with a movie that gets shown to sold-out audiences in theaters and has become a constant topic of conversation at home, in classrooms, in cafes, and at work. Like the *BILD-Zeitung* tabloid, whose high print runs only attest to its worthlessness, whose editors are reproached for opportunism, and whose readers are attributed with "false consciousness," it is the success of *Schindler's List* that makes the film so suspect in the eyes of critical intellectuals. Anything that draws in that many people just can't be good. As long as only innocuous products like *E.T.* or *Jurassic Park* are involved, the critics of the zeitgeist tolerate the phenomenon with elitist indifference. But when it comes to the "National Socialist genocide of the Jews and gypsies," then an aggressive desperation takes hold. "Really great works on the subject have failed inasmuch as they haven't reached the majority of the public," writes my Viennese friend Peter, and he concludes, "But we already knew that anyway: as enlighteners, we're hopeless." But rather than developing this astute observation further and asking why the "great works" haven't reached the public, Peter trashes these successful—though in his opinion low-quality—products like a frustrated music teacher whose students would rather listen to "Sergeant Pepper" than "Carmina Burana." "It probably lies in the nature of the event," he writes, "that the most cynical and trivial representations are the most successful. What artists unanimously agree to leave unmolested by realistic representation, film- and television-industry people ram point-blank into uniforms, barbed wire, every shot to the head a sure hit. And if you allow your conscience to be disturbed by the shameless banality of it, you'll only be told: But that's exactly how it was—Holocaust Lite. . . ."

If there were such a thing as an oath of disclosure for intellectuals, these statements would be accepted as a valid declaration of bankruptcy by every district court from St. Pölten to Winsen-an-der-Luhe. Actually, there hasn't been a "unanimous agreement" about what can or cannot be represented since the Third Reich's Imperial Culture Chamber, the Reichskulturkammer, closed up shop. But the "film- and television-industry people," who turn a profit on "shameless banality," must still be taken to task. A critic in the Berlin *Tagesspiegel* even wrote recently that "a lot of people are making a lot of money right now" on Spielberg's movie, which might lead an impartial reader to draw the hasty conclusion that the foes of opportunism and triviality practice their trade without compensation.

The objections raised by these intellectual linesmen to Spielberg's movie reflect above all the hopelessness of the official enlighteners, who now find themselves escaping into petty squabbles, where if nothing else they can test their competence at seeing details. One Viennese woman critic complained that the movie "fails to provide information regarding the causes of anti-Semitism"—as if it were the task of film to conduct that kind of research. If a critic were to denounce *Gone with the Wind* because Rhett Butler and Scarlett O'Hara had failed to explain the origins of the Civil War, he or she would make a fool of him- or herself.

But when it comes to Spielberg and Schindler, not a few heads can be seen nodding in agreement with the demand that the film be a seminar with visual aids rather than the telling of a story. And here, of course, every detail counts. Some academic-footnote fetishist discovered that a song sung in the movie in 1945 wasn't actually written until 1967 in Israel. Since then, the example has made the rounds as proof of Spielberg's "technical sloppiness." Such a tactic is hardly new. When "Nazis" showed up in Hollywood films of the 1960s and 1970s, German critics would always find something wrong with the details. Sometimes it was the color of the uniforms that was off, sometimes their caps hadn't been put on at the right angle, sometimes they sang songs that weren't even in the Wehrmacht songbook. Similarly, the inmates in Spielberg's camp appear too well-nourished and their haircuts entirely too stylish. Presumably even Jesus at the Last Supper did not look exactly the way Leonardo da Vinci would later paint him.

Bogus arguments like these make it clear that none of this has to do with the movie or even with the question of how a mass murder can be represented appropriately. It has to do with the fact that with *Schindler's List*, Spielberg has broken into the domain of those who up till now have had the monopoly on "mastering the past," who unself-consciously work the bloodbaths of yesterday into the feuilletons of today and the doctoral theses of tomorrow without giving a thought to "shameless banality." More than anything, dealing with the Holocaust used to be a pretty exclusive occupation. The experts–historians, psychologists, pedagogues–would meet each other at conferences and symposia organized like Harlem Globetrotters' games: the opponents came with them. Under pompous rubrics like "Memory for the Future" or "Genocide in the Industrial Age," they staged rigorous scholarly debates presenting to each other what they all had already copied down from the same sources and exchanged for reciprocal review. These exercises in applied redundancy were accompanied by well-meaning journalists and cooked up for posterity by sophisticated essayists. This is the milieu that produced many of the "great works" whose ineffectiveness my Viennese friend Peter bemoans.

And now: Spielberg. How does someone like that get involved with a subject like this? Has he studied history, genocide, and transportation? Does he have a classical humanist education, or did he get his degree from a college where they teach baseball? Aren't all Americans barbarians anyway, with a history that begins with General Custer and ends with General Schwarzkopf? And now one of them means to show us what the Holocaust was like? It's our Holocaust! We did it, we own the copyright for it, and no way are we transferring the subsidiary rights to anyone!

Germans would rather do without two days of paid vacation in favor of hospital insurance than share "their" Holocaust with anyone else. It doesn't matter that half the country can't stand hearing about it anymore; whole sections of the intellectual elite have found their spiritual home in the remnants of Auschwitz, and they refuse to be ousted, especially not by an American Jew who uses the gas chambers and crematoria as a movie set.

The philosopher Hermann Lübbe once spoke about the Germans' "pride in their sins." This attitude, coupled with the belief that business can only desecrate culture, drives the defenders of pure art to the barricades. Along with it comes a misunderstanding as German as a Loden coat and as outdated as a mechanical coffee grinder: you cannot enlighten and entertain at the same time; entertainment is only a way to pass, if not to waste, the time. And yet, entertainment is the only medium that can bind rational knowledge with emotional participation.

There is no way to look into the hearts and minds of cinema goers. No one can say what goes on inside people when they're watching Spielberg's film. A movie theater isn't a correctional facility, and no movie can keep pace with the reality it represents. But surely this much can be assumed: whoever goes to see *Schindler's List* will go home with an idea of what things were like. It's not much, but it's a lot more than what the "great works" of the hopelessly enlightened have accomplished.

*Translated by W. Martin*

# 10

## THE REPUBLIC OF SIMULATORS

All major airlines train their pilots in so-called flight simulators, which help to "simulate" a number of in-flight situations and potential hazards. The pilots learn what to do in case of an engine failure, a difficult approach into Hong Kong, or an emergency landing when the nose-wheel is disabled. And no pilot is allowed into the cockpit of an actual plane without first having put in a sufficient number of "flight hours" in a simulator. These practical apparatuses serve as ways of approximating reality; simulation is not a substitute for reality but a practical and safe method for coping with real situations.

In the case of the GDR, the opposite was true. People were prepared not for reality but for successful simulation. What mattered was not so much the approximation of the real but leaving the real world as far behind as possible. Even the creation of the GDR was a simulation of considerable originality: it was the first nation of workers and peasants on German soil and it had nothing at all to do with its predecessor, the NS regime. The founders of the GDR did not feel they shared responsibility for the Third Reich, nor was their Volk the same as that which until recently had comprised the masses of Volksgenossen.[1] The GDR's historical roots lay buried somewhere in the period of the Peasant Wars; then history took a huge leap, and the GDR fell from the sky along with the NVA, the VEBs, the Volkskammer, the Intershops along the transit highway, and the Getränkestützpunkte out in the country.[2] After that the simulation took off like there was no tomorrow. The government of the GDR simulated sovereignty; the Volkskammer simulated democracy; the Bloc parties simulated pluralism.[3] The unions simulated the representation of workers' interests; the people's own enterprises simulated productivity; the judiciary simulated autonomy; and the party, which was always right, simulated infallibility. That was already quite a lot, but you can't have too much of a good thing. The principle of simulation had to be cast over the entire country like a net. In a society whose biggest problem was the equal distribution of poverty, prosperity was simulated by falsifying statistics about the production of consumer goods. With the help of their slogan "Surpassing without Passing," they simulated a verifiable superiority over the capitalist West. At the same time, car buyers were being made to wait ten years for a Trabant, peas were being processed into marzipan, and green tomatoes into artificial lemon juice.

Much of what today comes across as merely provincial and middle-class is a result of the rigorous enforcement of the simulation principle. Specifically East German concepts like *Salatgarnitur, Gemüsevariation,* and *Sättigungs-beilage* weren't just unintentionally comical clichés.[4] They were the simulations of elegance, opulence, and culinary refinement. A linguistic monstrosity like "preventative antifascist rampart" pushed the simulation principle to its dialectical limit. Even though everyone knew that it was designed to forcibly prevent people from leaving the country, this structure was declared to be a defense measure against attack by external enemies. Whether those responsible for this phraseology believed in their fraud or not is completely irrelevant: the "preventative antifascist rampart" was a product of the simulation principle, as was the belief in its efficacy.

It goes without saying that such exercises can have degenerative consequences over time. The poets of Prenzlauer Berg[5] simulated a government-free zone while at the same time reporting the goings-on in their little biosphere to state agents. Helmut Eschwege describes an exceptionally remarkable case of simulation in his book *A Stranger to My Friends: Memoirs of a Dresden Jew.* In 1968, a woman whose father had belonged to an Einsatzgruppe, or task force, involved in the liquidation of the Jews, became the spokesperson for the Jewish community in the city of Halle. She had her parents buried in the row of honor in the Jewish cemetery and sent her son to Budapest for rabbinical schooling, only to have him sent home early for stealing books. The entire project took place with the knowledge and approval of Dr. Helmut Aris, an important functionary in the GDR Jewish community who had excellent ties to the state apparatus. Aris proved his own qualifications as a passive simulator by diligently overlooking GDR anti-Semitism and allowing himself to be hitched up to every propaganda wagon going by.

The false spokesperson of the Jewish community of Halle got herself a gold-letter entry in the Big East German Book of Simulators, but her case was hardly unique. Eschwege writes about a former NS stormtrooper who had managed to become the spokesperson of the Jewish community of Zittau, and he tells of Nazis who became members of the Coalition of the Victims of the NS Regime.

And when the end of the GDR came into view, the leading organs of the state and the party suddenly started simulating "philo-Semitism." Edgar Bronfman was invited on an official visit, and Heinz Galinski was awarded the Order of the Friendship of Peoples.[6] Firmly convinced of the power of "World Jewry," the last vestiges of the political outfit decided to polish the GDR's image in the United States with the help of some pro-Jewish smarm. And at the eleventh hour, in the fall of 1990, the GDR was even ready to establish diplomatic ties with Israel. A state that was about to vanish from the map was behaving for one last time as if it could conduct its foreign affairs with the same sense of sovereignty it maintained over its inner constitution.

In retrospect, one might ask if the GDR ever really existed, or if it was simply staged on a case-by-case basis. There's the famous "Protocol Route" in East Berlin that led to the government's guest quarters. The houses standing along it were painted and renovated as soon as a foreign visit was scheduled. Former GDR citizens can recall visits by Erich Honecker to especially chosen supermarkets that would be stocked with goods before the party chairman's arrival, only to be cleared out again after the state visit. It is impossible to speak of a "loss of reality" in cases like these, since it was well known what kind of reality there was. Everyone knew that while the facades on Sophienstrasse had been renovated, the courtyards behind them were falling apart. Everyone knew that the surplus was being simulated for a short time only, whereas under normal circumstances real coffee and decent toothpaste were nowhere to be found.

The simulation principle was universally applicable; it could be employed in any situation to produce what wasn't there and to make what was there go away. Internationalism, world-class status, and German-Soviet friendship were simulated in; racism, corruption, and prostitution were simulated out. No wonder that at some point in the course of time the East Germans misplaced a few critical standards. Being and seeming had been blended together into a thick, gooey mush whose elements were barely distinguishable anymore.

A professor of German at the University of Halle, Ingrid Kühn, has conducted a linguistic study of the code names of forty-five hundred Stasi IMs.[7] She stumbled upon an odd correspondence between the professional occupation of an IM and his choice of name. Doctors chose code names like "Albert Schweitzer," "Röntgen," or "Robert Koch." Philologists opted for "Goethe," "Schiller," or "Brecht." A choir director was transformed into IM "Beethoven," and a scholar of antiquities became IM "Ramses." "Leo," "Einstein," "Don Juan," and "Tannhäuser" all were favorite IM magic caps, making their wearer's dreams come true. The difficulties that many former IMs have with their past as freelancers for the Stasi could very well stem from the fact that they themselves no longer know when they were simulating and when they were appearing "authentically." Did IM "Secretary" simulate a Stasi agent in the church, or a cleric in the Stasi? Or is he today only simulating a Social Democratic minister president who speaks of himself in the third person like a feudal lord?[8]

At the end of September 1989, that is, only days before the collapse of the GDR, Manfred Stolpe wrote in *Der Spiegel*, "The principal direction of history today is not the establishment of a Greater Germany but collective peacekeeping efforts in Europe and the entire world. Humanity no longer has any choice but collective survival or collective demise." A few paragraphs later, he asks whether "the government and all the other parties in the Federal Republic . . . intend to hammer away at reunification until all we're left with is shards. . . ." But anyone with eyes and ears could see that in the GDR they were clamoring for political unification. Were the Monday Demonstrations merely processions of simulators?[9] And if the alternatives were either "collective survival or collective demise," then why did Stolpe's countrymen waste so much time quibbling over exchange rates for their savings?

It's easy to understand that for a person who has founded his whole existence on simulation, a sudden confrontation with the "real reality" will present a serious shock. A pilot who has never left his flight simulator, who has never had anything but mock takeoffs, mock landings, and mock turbulence but who is nevertheless convinced of the reality of these simulated maneuvers, would immediately have to make a crash landing if he had to fly an actual plane. This is exactly what has happened to the East Germans since reunification. Hardly had they left their people's own antifascist plasto- and elasto-universal simulator when they felt hoodwinked, abused, and colonized. Although the demonstrations for reunification took place in East Berlin, Leipzig, and Dresden, and not in Aachen, Hildesheim, or Kaufbeuren, everyone started talking about an Anschluß. The dreaded Stasi, the incarnation of all evil between the Elbe and the Oder, was suddenly transformed into a "guarantor of internal freedom" (Peter Michael Diestel, last minister of the interior and acting minister president of the GDR). The last minister of the interior for the GDR, during whose administration a large part of the Stasi files was destroyed, recently posed the question "whether conformity in the context of a dictatorship could be considered criminal or not." He immediately provided a fitting response: "After all, we can't go on forever depicting the GDR as an outlaw state."

This is clearly a case of the words being just as crooked as the thought is warped–an intellectual counterpart to the physical efforts of the citizens of Rostock-Lichtenhagen toward a peaceful coexistence with their foreign fellow citizens.[10] If you don't want to depict the GDR as an outlaw state, then you don't have to bring up the issue of conformity under dictatorship. If it is brought up, though, then we should ask ourselves who the conformers were and to whom were they conforming; that is, who profited, and how, from the dictatorship. Only someone who has elevated simulation to a general principle will consider his own conformity under dictatorship to have been an act of passive resistance while retrospectively editing out the "positive sides" of life in a closed institution. Heiner Müller, who simulated the intellectual cynic for as long as he himself was never in the hot seat, frequently remarked that life under dictatorship was more inspiring for an artist than it would be in a democracy. Simpler souls like the well-known television interviewer Günter Gaus still get excited over the "niche society" and the "human warmth" it generated, when really it was at most a by-product of the fug that develops whenever the kitchen windows haven't been opened in a while.

But hardly anyone has mastered the fine art of simultaneously simulating both the past and the present as well as Regine Hildebrandt. As minister of social services in Brandenburg, she owes her reputation as a committed advocate of the disenfranchised and disadvantaged to two circumstances: her being a woman, and her ability to talk without having to breathe. She won't, she tells us every chance she gets, shed a single tear for the GDR. But it would be good if at least a few of the "social accomplishments of the GDR" could be adopted. At which point everyone thinks of Kindergärten, grüner Pfeil, and Muttermilchsammelstellen and nods in agreement.[11] There's no point then in considering whether the GDR's social accomplishments weren't as inextricably bound up with its political system as were the Winterhilfswerk and Kraft durch Freude programs with the apparatus of National Socialism.[12] The social commitment that Regine Hildebrandt embodies and that makes her so insanely popular is of a piece with the self-satisfied antifascism of the GDR, whose proponents inebriated themselves on the sound of their own words. The slightly down-at-heels historical subject, back from the manhunt in Rostock, and the minister who protects his social welfare have one thing in common: they both feel like victims of foreign intervention and are utterly convinced that they have been forced into a situation for which they are not responsible.

And so, with transversed plus and minus signs, the simulation continues on its merry way. In reaction to the post-GDR outbreak of right-wing radicalism, Hans Modrow, the last minister president of the GDR, made a public announcement in Berlin: "Despite everything for which my involvement in the party makes me accountable and deserving of reproach, I will never apologize for my antifascism to anyone!" As if someone had actually asked him to. Encouraged by the thunderous applause, he added: "I see nothing wrong in the fact that antifascism was the *raison d'état* of the GDR. In fact, I wish it were still that way!" Although the consequences of simulated antifascism can be seen everywhere from Hoyerswerda to Rostock, with its accompanying "raison d'état" still being upheld, the simulation principle remains in effect.

IM "Heiner," a.k.a. Heiner Fink, the interim rector of the Humboldt-Universität during the Wende, announced at the inaugural meeting of the "Committee for Justice" that he was thinking of calling himself Heinrich "Stasi" Fink from now on. He wanted to demonstrate that the same thing was being done to him that was done to the Jews during the Third Reich, when they had to refer to themselves as "Sarah" and "Israel." Christa Wolf, who simply "forgot" about her collaboration with the Stasi, compares her situation to the fate of the Jewish artists and intellectuals who were driven out of Germany. Just as Germany then had "rid itself of left-wing and Jewish culture," so does it now "disclaim the culture we had in the GDR." An East Berlin weekly, *Die Weltbühne,* has denounced the "inquisitional orgies of disclosure" led by the "self-appointed organs for the formation of a national morality." This is correct only insofar as morality formation in the GDR also depended on the approval of political organs; and "self-appointed" moral authorities were either put in prison or kicked out of the country.

The right to free speech entails the right to ethical self-disembowelment. That applies to both the East and the West. The simulation principle will prove to be an extremely useful metasystemic bond, the least common denominator between participants in the new German unity. Now that everyone knows how in the West the will to reunification was simulated for decades, it will soon become clear that the present "reappraisal of GDR history" is being simulated, too. Where once the FDGO[15] and the first nation of workers and peasants on German soil coexisted side by side, now the republic of simulators is settling in.

*Translated by W. Martin*

## TRANSLATOR'S NOTES

1. *Volksgenossen:* national comrade. This is a NS appellation for "citizen," but Broder is clearly calling attention to the GDR's continued and unqualified usage of both *Volk* and *Genosse.*

2. *Nationale Volksarmee* (NVA): National People's Army; *Volkseigener Betrieb* (VEB): People's Own Enterprise; *Volkskammer:* parliament (literally, "The People's Chamber"); *Intershop:* hard currency shop; *transit highway:* highways where regular traffic between the Federal Republic and West Berlin was permitted; *Getränkestützpunkte:* beverage posts (small shops selling refreshments and sundries).

3. Bloc parties (Blockpartien) were nonoppositional political parties permitted by the ruling Soziale Einheits Partei (SED), or Socialist Unity party.

4. *Salatgarnitur:* salad garnish; *Gemüsevariation:* mixed vegetables; *Sättigungsbeilage:* side dish.

5. A neighborhood in (East) Berlin.

6. Edgar Bronfman, the president of the World Jewish Congress and chairman of the Seagram Company, Ltd.; Heinz Galinski, spokesperson for the Jewish community in Germany.

7. *Stasi:* Staatssicherheitdienst (State Security Service). "IM" is an abbreviation for Informelle Mitarbeiter (informal collaborator).

8. Broder is referring to Manfred Stolpe, the Prime Minister of Brandenburg who resigned in 2002.

9. A series of demonstrations held in Leipzig in October 1989, which led directly to the opening of the Wall the following month.

10. Broder is referring to events of August 1992, in which right-wing radical Germans burned down the homes of foreign asylum seekers and Vietnamese guest workers in the Rostock neighborhood of Lichtenhagen.

11. *Kindergärten:* day care centers; *grüner Pfeil:* green arrow (the traffic signal permitting a right turn on red); and *Muttermilchsammelstellen:* breast milk collection stations (a social service for exchanging breast milk among nursing mothers).

12. *Winterhilfswerk:* winter relief works (NS social welfare organization); *Kraft durch Freude:* strength through happiness (NS leisure organization).

13. FDGO (Freiheitlich demokratische Grundordnung): the Liberal Democratic Order. This was the political-philosophical idea legitimizing the West German constitution, in contrast to the Marxist-Leninist principles that were invoked by the GDR to legitimize their constitution.

## OSTALGIA:

## THE GDR IS BACK

The geographic center of the GDR is situated at twelve degrees, thirty-one minutes eastern longitude and fifty-two degrees, twelve minutes northern latitude, near the town of Verlorenwasser in the Potsdam-Mittelmarkt district, halfway between the restaurant Zur Hirschtränke and the bed and breakfast Jagdhaus Weitzgrund. Up until the Wende, the spot, marked by a sign in the woods, was a popular destination for day trips. There was a lot of boozing and carrying-on around the "Center"–even if in an almost dissident manner– especially on Ascension Day, known as *Herrentag* in the GDR. "After Ascension Day was abolished as a holiday," Klaus Nichelmann recalls, "we had to submit vacation requests six months in advance before the management realized what day it was."

With the end of the GDR, stillness also descended on the "Center of the GDR" until Klaus Nichelmann, spokesman for the "Pro-Belzig" citizens' initiative, became active. He had a wooden pavilion built only a few meters from the original spot, with a sign reading, "Attention: This Is the Center of the Former GDR!" The celebrations took place again on Ascension Day 1995, still called

*Herrentag*, with Wernesgrüner Beer and soup ladled from goulash barrels. In addition, Nichelmann brought a fourteen-by-four-centimeter stamp, so every participant in the celebration could receive certification that he had visited the "Center of the Former GDR." Some people brought their old GDR ID cards to be stamped.

A strange phenomenon is spreading between Cape Arkona to the north and Apolda to the south: the GDR is back. The Workers' and Peasants' State is gone, yet the country still (or once again) rotates on its own axis. It's similar for the people who suddenly became homeless without ever leaving their living rooms. "I lived here, it wasn't all bad," says Klaus Nichelmann, and immediately adds that he wouldn't have the SED and the Politburo back for anything in the world. "People didn't really get the Wende, and afterwards everyone was busy adjusting to all of the changes. It's only now that we're getting around to reflecting on it."

Nichelmann, born in East Prussia in 1943, mobilized with his citizens' initiative to make Belzig the district seat. Now, the heating engineer, who became self-employed after the Wende, devotes all of his free time to maintaining the "Center." This is, he says, "everyday lived history." A big folk festival is planned for the millenial anniversary celebration of Belzig. Until then, Nichelmann hopes that the reactivated "Center of the Former GDR" will become known as a tourist attraction far beyond the boundaries of district seat Belzig.

Worlds lie between the patch in the woods near Verlorenwasser and the concrete wastes of Prenzlauer Berg, yet the people here are driven by the same need as the people there: to submerge themselves in history so they can experience it once more.

Every Friday at ten o'clock the "ost rock test the west disco" fires up in the former canteen of the KulturBrauerei. Here too the GDR is reconstructed to scale for a couple of hours. "The music comes from the East, the cover charge is *authentic* East, and so are the drinks," says Uwe, thirty-three, a skilled electrician, who together with his friend Peter, a thirty-two-year-old pastry chef, has stood behind the counter for one night a week and played bartender. The cover charge, just like in the former GDR, is 3.10 East Marks; a glass of vodka and cola (prepared with the People's Own Club Cola) is 3.0 East Marks. Those who would rather drink beer reach for *authentic* East labels like Radelberger, Wernesgrüner, and Bürgerbräu. Axel and Udo, the DJs, mix the music in accordance with an old regulation of the GDR Ministry of Culture, 60:40—meaning that 60 percent of the titles played have to be GDR productions. "Music we used to like listening to," Uwe says and puts his guest from the West to the test by rattling off a few names: "Pankow, Karat, Holgar Biege, Ute Freundenberg." The DJ has just put on the "Gänselied" by Klaus Renft. "It's not just the music, it's the collective memory. When the *Gänselied* plays they all look at each other and they just know without saying a thing."

With their thirty-plus years, Uwe and Axel have some seniority in this packed, cranked, smoky space. Most of the visitors to Friday night's "ost rock test the west disco" at the KulturBrauerei are under twenty-five years old. A few years ago these kids would blow a whole week's wages on a pair of authentic Wrangler jeans, they would have traded their FDJ card for an old Udo Lindenburg CD, and today it can't be "zoney" enough for them.

Uwe doesn't understand why his guest is so surprised and recommends that I come back when the old GDR films are shown in the "Boiler House": *Heißer Sommer* or *Die Legende von Paul und Paula*.[1] "Then everybody sits there, hugging each other and bawling."

"The further back the Wende gets, the better the GDR looks," says Ralf Scherff, thirty-two, who runs the Kaufmannsladen, or "Salesman's Store," in Berlin-Mitte with his brother Andreas, thirty-three. The two still stock a couple of original GDR articles, for example, Grabower Kisses ("Chocolate Kisses with Glaze Containing Cocoa") and Dr. Quendt ABCD Russian bread ("Quality You Can Taste"). The Club-Cola, says Ralf, "tastes just like it used to," even though the label has been redesigned. More and more customers come into the store, see an old brand name, and exclaim, "The East is back! Great!"

Behind the counter Ralf has put up a "Price Board, Price Level II" from an old HO restaurant,[2] a reminder of the times when a half-pint of Deutsches Pilsner cost exactly fifty-one Pfennigs, a shot of Weizendoppelkorn cost seventy-three Pfennigs, and a bottle of Kräuterbitterlikör cost sixty Pfennigs. Ralf was trained to do automotive bodywork and then signed on to play bit parts at the Deutsches Theater. He always "did his own thing," like buying signs from old businesses and leather jackets in the provinces and selling them in Berlin. Somehow he always got by. "The GDR was the state of perpetual exceptions, life made people sick. And people who didn't take the time to recover stayed sick." In 1988 he refused the draft and would have "certainly landed in jail if it weren't for the Wende." Nevertheless, he says, "I wouldn't want to miss a single day from the GDR. We had so much fun, experienced so many beautiful things."

And because working at the store isn't enough for him, he organizes events, most recently the "Schwalbe Festival Berlin," a meeting of connoisseurs of the GDR motor scooters of the legendary Simson make. "We didn't want the Westerners to lead us by the hand. This is *our* past."

The Ossi, that enigmatic being: first he can't get rid of the GDR fast enough, then he laments its loss, and finally tries to piece it back together from a few fragments. While the necessity of "internal unity" is the talk of the West, the

East sets itself at an increasing distance from the West the more that their living conditions converge. Back when you could easily tell an Ossi because he said "Hamse?" instead of "haben Sie?" and "Plaste" instead of "Plastik," he wanted to be just like his West German cousin: cool, astute, and aloof. Now that he can discern Benetton from Ralph Lauren and Nike from Reebok, he reflects on his own, unmistakable identity. He drives a Trabbi again, he smokes F6 and Club,[3] drinks Goldbrand and Nordhäuser Doppelkorn. And when he goes to the Mokka-Milch-Eisbar on East Berlin's Karl Marx Boulevard, reopened in 1995 and until 1990 *the* ice cream shop in the East German capital, he likes to order the Pittiplatsch (fruity ice cream, whipped cream, peaches, and chocolate jimmies) or the "Swedish Sunday" (vanilla ice cream, whipped cream, advocaat, and apple sauce), two delicacies typical of the GDR. Among the more proper entrees, at least two classics of GDR cuisine top the charts: Soljanka and spiced meat. "Recently we offered cream of avocado soup. No one wanted it," says the boyfriend of the proprietress, who was allowed to leave the GDR after spending two years in Niederschönhausen Prison for attempting to flee the Republic illegally in 1981 and has been living in the West ever since. Another hit that was often played in the seventies on GDR Radio belongs to the acoustic ambiance of the Mokka-Milch-Eisbar: "In the Mokka-Milch-Eisbar / she saw me standing there / in the Mokka-Milch-Eisbar / yes that was where." The reopening in March 1995 was attended by Thomas Natschinski, who recorded the song with his group over twenty years ago.

"In 1990, the West was suddenly everywhere," says the twenty-four-year-old East Berliner Petra. "We had no time to really say goodbye to the GDR–it took a while before we understood what had happened."

Five years later, many former citizens of the GDR make their way through a virtual GDR reality in order to experience it anew, this time deliberately and without haste. The Stufe 85 gallery[4] on the fifth floor of an East Berlin factory building shows "Rarities, Kitsch, and Curiosities from the GDR," a gruesomely beautiful collection of political posters ("The Way We Work Today Is the Way We Will Live Tomorrow"), pennants ("We're Fighting for the Title of Socialist Work Brigade!"), and slogans ("Surpassing without Passing!" "Tips Not Accepted!"), rounded off with artifacts of everyday socialist life: among other things, a cuddly teddy bear in an NVA uniform,[5] a gigantic mural from the Central Council of the FDJ,[6] handicrafts from an anti-imperialist solidarity bazaar, a sign saying "Border Zone" in German, English, French, and Russian, on the back of which someone had painted "Fresh Eggs to Give Away," a shopping bag containing a packet of Spee laundry detergent, a pound of Magdeburger egg noodles, a pack of gauze, and a packet of peppermint candies from the VEB Combine Oschersleben Sweets.[7] A cot of Soviet make hangs on the wall ("To

Learn from the Soviet Union Is to Learn to Lie Down!"); a vacuum cleaner of the Steppke make stands in the corner; next to it is an NVA mat ("For Our Security!"), depicting a girl in the uniform of the Young Pioneers handing a bouquet of red roses to a Kalashnikov-wielding soldier–a legion of examples from the repository of a closed state theater.

For opening night, an event called Finissage, about a hundred people come to discuss the theme of the exhibit, "No Time for Goodbyes." First Ilona Seffner, forty, who runs the Stufe 85 gallery under the auspices of an ABM project for "social culture,"[8] reads a few of her poems. They are, she says, "not so much poems as descriptions of certain attitudes." One of her ditties is called "My GDR" and goes like this:

> GDR, home of my heart
> Oh how distant thou art,
> Your walls and your towers,
> The old men in your bowers.
> I feel torn to splinters,
> My eyes by time embittered,
> Not a chance has been laid,
> what is worse,
> you make me afraid.

Then Ilona Seffner tells of how on the day the Wall fell, a neighbor came to her and said, "the border is open," and they both sat down and wept; how she went with her son for the first time to the West; how her knees went weak at the border, and she almost vomited from the excitement. "It was a slow-motion film–an incredible intensity."

And then Ilona Seffner, who worked as an educator in the GDR, directed a project for at-risk youth in Prenzlauer Berg after the Wende, and subsequently spent a year and a half on unemployment, reads a few more of her poems, among them one entitled "The People's Decision":

> Now it is done.
> The people's power has won.
> Socialism set asunder.
> The SED six feet under.
> Finally, our own paradise.
> And already tears well in my eyes.

In a poem titled "Identity Crisis," she laments the "weight of the loss" that she has experienced–"Forcefully united with the trash heap of the West." In "Farewell to My Country," it goes: "I'll show you my sadness / Even if it drives you to madness / Because you blew away a great chance." The closing discussion isn't, as one might surmise, about the quality of Ilona Seffner's poetry but rather the exhibit's theme, "No Time for Goodbyes." It is supposed to "lead out of the chaos," says Peter Finke, a former research associate at the Institute for Pedagogical Psychology of the Academy of Pedagogical Sciences of the GDR, one of the exhibition's sponsors. "It's time to finally move beyond the things that we have experienced. Both memory and letting go of memories help that."

"Stop!" a woman shouts back. "Don't talk like you're the majority, don't say 'we.' I don't want to move beyond it, it's part of my life and that has substance."

A man who introduces himself as a musician and top-forty songwriter says that he never "encountered political propaganda in daily life"; if a West German came to this exhibit, all his stereotypes about the GDR would be confirmed. There were of course "countercultures" in the GDR, but these were wholly absent from the exhibit.

If it hadn't driven people to tears, they could have laughed about daily life in the GDR, says a former GDR citizen. "That's something I already felt then. I parted gladly with these kinds of things—I don't miss them."

The exhibit is one-sided, complains one young woman. She "misses the other side of the GDR," the presentation of the positive things that were also there: "I don't need party banners or FDJ banners, I don't mourn for them."

"You're just wallowing in the muck of your memories! Why are you doing this?" a male visitor yells from the background. Peter Finke reacts a little impatiently: "I can't accept that. We lived here like totally ordinary citizens. We had a relatively normal life that could be compared to the life of a citizen in the Federal Republic if you left aside specific freedoms like the right to travel and freedom of consumption. There's no reason to talk about muck!"

At this point a visitor from the West interjects with the observation that there can be no talk about a normal life "when I don't have the option of informing myself on anything but official opinion." The Ossis immediately close ranks. One must be "a little careful" with questions of freedom, as the visitor from the West is informed by Renaldo Tolksdörfer, a former FDJ secretary who today sells "GDR devotionals and books," which he collected from the library of the SED Party School and the gift stocks of the State Council just after the Wende. "In the GDR I'd get sent up to Bautzen prison if I said Honecker is an idiot. On the other hand, I *could* say that my manager wasn't playing with a full deck because he didn't provide a warm meal for the night shift. Today it's the other way around. They can say that Kohl's not quite right in the head, but let them say that about their boss and they're out on the street like that." Until November 1989, Tolksdörfer explains, he had the feeling of "living well in the GDR." That isn't a question of feelings, counters the guest from the West, but rather of "objective options that one has or one doesn't" and that are "also objectively ascertainable."

"We had everything you had," Peter Finke asserts with categorical certainty, "it was all just a little smaller. The car, the washing machine, the refrigerator, the TV." And he shows no signs of irritation as a woman interrupts, yelling: "that's absolutely untrue!"

These are therapeutic discussions that ex-GDR citizens hold about their lives in the former GDR. They get started by a Mitropa cup or an FDJ pennant and lead straight to "mental states" of an existence full of contradictions, insults, and compromises. The visitors' reactions, says Ilona Seffner, range from, "I want the GDR back, everything was better there" to, "this is unbearable, why do we do this to ourselves?" An SED slogan, a poster for the Society for German-Soviet Friendship, a plastic vase from a solidarity bazaar all evoke memories "that many have repressed and denied." No one from the West can relate to "what played out with us," this "mixture of welfare and stupidity, of order and improvisation."

This type of confrontation with one's own history only functions when the Ossis are among themselves. The appearance of a Wessi brings out immediate and defensive counterreactions. As soon as the Ossis come to the understanding among themselves that the "GDR's stench" was actually unbearable, the Wessi question, "How did you stand it?" summons the "good side" of the GDR to the fore; something like the Social Insurance book, which every citizen in the GDR had and which contained "everything you needed for retirement."

What is somewhat hastily referred to as "Ostalgia" in the West plays itself out at flea markets, where GDR flags, toy Trabbis, and SED pins are sold. In "Newfiveland," Ostalgia often has very practical and comprehensible foundations. "I waited twelve years for this car; it's a bonding experience," a woman from Brandenburg replies to the question of why she still drives a Trabbi when she could have bought a real car years ago.

"People have to understand the connection between shopping and jobs—if they are only buying West products, they can't be surprised that businesses are closing in the East," says Pierre Gedalge, who, together with his partner, Harald Kujus, has opened a supermarket in the East Berlin district of Friedrichshain with the name Zurück in die Zukunft, or "Back to the Future." The two aim to draw over fifty percent of their returns from the sale of East products, which for them is anything made in the East, even though many firms have since come under Western ownership. The selection runs from Elmenhorster fruit juices from Rostock and Rhone Drop bitters from Meiningen to

Pasewaler preserves and Möwe Fine egg noodles from Waren-on-Müritz to Würzner corn flakes, Burger Crackers, and Werra-Krepp toilet paper from Wernshausen in Thuringia.

"I have two kids, a dog, property, and a loan out–this is also about my job," says Gedalge, who was born two weeks after the Wall was erected and became self-employed in 1990 with a fruit and vegetable shop. He explains the logical consideration behind the name of his store as "back to the products of the past and therefore into the future."

In fact, the ostalgic preoccupation with the GDR resembles a flight into the past and into the future at once. No one would have guessed before the Wende that the Trabbi, the symbol for the economy of scarcity and cramped comfort, would, in the nineties, advance to the status of a cult car, seen as worthy objects of collectors, who actually speculate in their value as collectibles.

And no one could have predicted that East Berlin youth, who stormed the western part of the city en masse in November 1989, would today prefer to remain among each other in locales like the Tagung in Wühlischstraße, with the bust of Marchlovski transformed into a barstool, where coffee is served in real Mitropa cups, and there's a blue menu from the Twelfth FDJ Parliament stating, "The Tagung Collective Wishes You Bon Appetite!" The guests are alerted to what they can expect upon entering the bar by a placard: "Mon.: Shipping and Receiving; Tues.: Vacation or Sick Day; Wed.: Inventory; Thurs.: Barber Shop and Beauty Day; Fri.: Back in Ten Minutes; Sat.: Brigade Party; Sun.: Day of Rest."

Or the Mauerblümchen, or "Wall Flower," cafe on Wisbyer Straße. A chunk of the Wall made of Styrofoam hangs over the bar, right next to a blue cardboard suitcase once used by a delegate to the Tenth Parliament of the FDJ in June 1976. Of the many decorations, both of the proprietors take pride in two: a dark metal sign, of which there was only one: "Magistrate of Berlin–Capital of the GDR," and the last "Certificate for the Release from Citizenship of the German Democratic Republic," from November 13, 1989. Naturally, they have *Soljanka* ("the Week in Review") and the Griletta ("King of Cheeseburgers!") to eat and champagne with pineapple to drink. "It's unbelievable how quickly people forget what it was like to live then," says Jens Ramble, co-owner of Mauerblümchen. "The Ossis can laugh at themselves here, and the Wessis can learn something about the GDR."

This could also be Peter Sodann's didactic intention, if he had one. The director of the New Theater in Halle debuted a Revue 60 right after the Wende, which has since been staged before a full house many times over. It is a recreation of the GDR in the sixties done in the form of a historical collage. What was once bitterly serious and official truth is now served up word for word by an ironical hand. The heroes of the Workers' and Peasants' State are just waiting to be outed as comedians.

Walter Ulbricht explains again that no one has any intention of building a wall, and shortly thereafter, following the successful building of that wall, he reports that during these "eventful days, much less has happened than at a rock and roll show in Berlin." Then he promises that by 1965 the socialist camp will have achieved a surplus of foodstuffs; the FDJ choir sings "We Are Everywhere on the Earth"; Ulbricht dances with Khrushchev while two young pioneers sing "We Never Want to Break Up"; the Bloc party representatives praise the leading role of the SED; the workers' choir from the VEB Chemical Works Bund sings "From the ovens, from the convoys, we have won our joy!"; farmers at an LPG in the Halle District write Walter Ulbricht that he can trust them to build socialism;[9] an activist yells, "If for our future you give a jerk, then be a Gagarin when you're at work!" The whole ensemble participates in the Hafenkonzert von Konstanza, or "Harbor Concert of Konstanza"; women workers display clothing for the "socialist daily life of our women"; farmers, artists, and workers submit declarations of loyalty; a choir of girls trills "we love the homeland, so beautiful, and we protect it because it belongs to the people."

The theater is transformed into an SED party hall for the performance. The "delegates" sit at long white-covered tables decorated with red flags, the walls are adorned with flags for the GDR, the SED, the FDJ, the FDGB, and the Society for German-Soviet Friendship.[10] Below hang portraits of the members of the Politburo. It's been a long time since the citizens of the GDR have experienced their country as authentically as at the Revue 60. For two hours the Ulbricht era struggles to its feet like a zombie.

"Do we remember the way IT was then, the way WE were then? Let us gather for a great Party Day to celebrate ten years of Socialism in practice. But this time for your entertainment, not your edification," runs the description in *Der Hammer*, the official publication of the New Theater.

At the first performances shortly after the Wende there were those who did not wish to be entertained. "They ran out, because they thought the show was a mockery of the GDR," recalls Peter Sodann, who has been a theater director in Halle since 1981. Since then no one runs out mid-show. "There's a powerful interest in the past. We want to know how it was. And just how stupid were we? How did we let ourselves get burned?" Yet Sodann also denies that Revue 60 is an effort to create distance from the GDR. "Sure, it's true that we even found some things in our lives pleasant. Life in the GDR was difficult, but funny, the lifestyle over here was more interesting. I'm not hanging on to anything. I'm hanging on to my life. And this is where I worked—before you could have said 'fought.' This is where I was locked up—and I do hang on to that somehow."

Sodann spent nine months in custody awaiting trial in 1961 after he staged a program called "Wo Der Hund begraben liegt" (loosely translated: Where Dead Dogs Lie) by the Leipzig cabaret Rat der Spötter, or "Council of Sartirists." Was the GDR an amusement park for artists and intellectuals? "Maybe, but one where you could get hurt very easily."

Now the adventure can be relived without risk of injury. Sodann tells of how he founded a party group with two other prisoners in jail; how he left the Society for German-Soviet Friendship after June 17 but then rejoined, because otherwise he could not have ridden motorcycles in the Society for Sport and Technology; how in the GDR people tried to outwit the frequency jammers with the help of a device called a "Russian Killer." And he remembers how in the GDR days young people came to him and complained about how boring it was. "I told them: go to your party secretary and tell him that you want to join the party. Then they'll take you. And finally you'll say whatever it is you think, and they'll throw you out. Then life'll get interesting."

Experiences that no Wessi can comprehend. And even a real Ossi like Peter Sodann, born in Meißen in 1936, a trained toolmaker, graduate of the Dresden Workers' and Peasants' College, and student of Helene Weigel at the Berliner Ensemble, thinks about times gone by with a mixture of whimsy and relief. "I'm glad that it's happened like it did and that the GDR has become history."

And not to be "misunderstood," he quickly makes another thing clear: "nobody wants the GDR back, but no one wants it taken away either."

*Translated by Hunter Bivens*

**TRANSLATOR'S NOTES**

1. *Heißer Sommer,* or *Hot Summer,* was a teen beach musical released in 1968 by DEFA, the GDR film studio. *Die Legende von Paul und Paula,* or *The Legend of Paul and Paula,* released in 1972, was one of DEFA's few attempts at the aesthetics of psychedelia and has achieved a certain cult status.

2. HO stands for Handels Organisation, or Trade Organization, the term for state-owned trading concerns in the GDR.

3. F6 and Club were two brands of cigarettes in the GDR, now considered the choice of price-conscious smokers in the Berlin Republic.

4. *Stufe 85* could translate to Level 85 or Step 85, as in the eighty-fifth step in the staircase.

5. Nationale Volksarmee, or the National People's Army, was the designation of the GDR military.

6. FDJ stands for *Freie Deutsche Jugend,* or Free German Youth, which was the mass organization for the youth of the GDR.

7. Volkseigener Betrieb, or People's Own Enterprise, was the designation of GDR industrial concerns.

8. ABM stands for *Arbeitsbeschaffungsmaßnahmen,* or job creation measures, a federally subsidized "welfare to work"–type program for the "chronically unemployed."

9. LPG stands for Landschaftswirtliche Produktionsgenossenschaft, or Agricultural Co-operative, in other words, a collective farm.

10. The Freier Deutscher Gewerkschaftsbund, or Free German Trade Union Federation, was the state-sponsored trade union in the GDR.

## THE GERMANIZATION

## OF THE HOLOCAUST

I was rather taken aback when I read an article about the Americanization of the Holocaust in an American periodical a few years ago. I was even more surprised to subsequently experience the intensity of Americans' preoccupation with the Holocaust in situ. They have two national Holocaust museums, with a third in the works, and almost every city has its own Holocaust memorial. At universities from coast to coast, students can take classes in something called "Holocaust Studies"—although the name makes it hard to tell whether the discipline is designed to teach how to organize a Holocaust or how to avert one. At well-attended dinners and luncheons honoring Holocaust survivors, their wealthy descendents donate money for memorials and raise funds for future fundraisers. A naive observer might conclude that the Nazi Holocaust took place in the United States of America and that Americans feel obligated to come to grips with this dark chapter of their history.

This kind of historical-heritage hunting calls for a counteroffensive that speaks in terms of the "Germanization of the Holocaust." There's no way around it: we must firmly establish that we own the historical copyright on this concept, just like we hold the international copyright on the terms *Kindergarten,* *Kaffeeklatsch, Weltanschauung, Doppelgänger, Schadenfreude, Poltergeist, Angst,* and *Ersatz.* When speaking of the "Germanization of the Holocaust," I'm not referring merely to the copyright of an idea but rather to the process of internalization and the marketing approach. As the historian Christian Meier has noted, Germans have been reminded of Auschwitz so often that the death camps have become an integral component of our self-image.

It wasn't always like this. In the fifties and sixties Germans wanted nothing to do with the Holocaust. The mass murder of the Jews had faded into the abyss of German history along with the Third Reich. If anyone nevertheless made reference to "those years," it was only to correct exaggerations or misrepresentation, arguing, generally, that you shouldn't foul the nest. Besides, there wasn't a single person or party participant in the war who hadn't committed horrific crimes. Even well into the seventies, there were serious debates about whether the Jewish civilians murdered by the Nazis shouldn't be seen as "combatants." After all, hadn't Chaim Weizmann written Neville Chamberlain in August of 1939, on behalf of the Zionist World Congress, suggesting that the Jews would align themselves with Great Britain and the other democratic allies? Couldn't that be seen as a sort of "declaration of war," and wouldn't that confer the Nazis the right to deal with the Jews accordingly?

In 1979, when the U.S. miniseries *Holocaust* aired on German television, the Germans reacted like startled children who'd just been told they came from another planet. The newspapers were replete with regrets: Those defending themselves with "We knew nothing," and those conceding, "Of course, we knew, but we didn't want to have anything to do with it." Up to that point, the Holocaust had been the exclusive province of a small circle of experts focused mostly on the question of whether or not Hitler himself had issued the order for the Final Solution to the Jewish Question.

Since the mid-1980s the situation has changed drastically. Dealing with the Holocaust has become a sort of popular national sport in which neither revisionists nor Holocaust deniers are on the opponent's team. On the contrary, every newspaper article, every radio program, every TV documentary, and every book covering this issue begins by concluding that the Holocaust is singular and unique, incomparable to any other mass murder or act of genocide in the history of humanity. The eleventh commandment has gone into effect: Thou shalt not compare! Whoever speaks, as the writer Peter Schneider has, in terms of "concentration camps" in the former Yugoslavia, whoever dares compare, structurally and systematically, as I sometimes do, the GDR with the Third Reich is side-barred on the spot: trivializing the Third Reich with such comparisons is in contempt of court!

Theories about how dealing with the Holocaust could have gone from anathema to national anthem vary. One possible explanation is that, by the mid-1980s, most of the perpetrator generation had died out, and the generation of forty-somethings could afford to pose historical questions without having to reckon with rebuttals: so who was the former owner of the Steinway piano you inherited from your parents?

And so it was that in an incredibly short period of time an even more incredible paradigmatic shift occurred. It used to go something like this: To hell with Auschwitz! Look at the havoc the French wreaked in Algeria, the British in South Africa, the Dutch in Indonesia, the Italians in Libya, and the Americans in the Wild West. Today, though, it's more like this: Let's just see someone try to have a Holocaust the likes of ours. The philosopher Hermann Lübbe speaks of the "German Sündenstolz," or "pride of sin," referring in these terms to an attitude that is without parallel in the history of Germany. The silence of the guilty conscience has been supplanted by a cultural surplus production that feeds on the consciousness of having accomplished something singular, unsurpassable, and inimitable. Let other people take pride in inventing striptease, thermoses, and compact discs; we invented the Holocaust!

Of course, no German in his right mind would ever say: The Holocaust was a splendid event, a proud part of our cultural heritage! What he does say, though, is: No one in the world has a history as horrific as ours, and no one has learned as much from their history as we have—no one has drawn such deep insights from the past as we. And so German pacifists, resting their case on German history, would rather examine every other incidence of genocide in the world than agree to send a few German paramedics in to help the victims. And so German newspapers warn the Israelis against making the same mistakes with Palestine as the Germans made in their dealings with the Jews. Not only as shysters but as consultants the Germans can't be beat! Because, of course, it takes a violent criminal to understand the criminal mind.

A young neo-Nazi who dissociates himself from the milieu and writes his memoirs is guaranteed a bestseller and invitations to appear on one talk show after another. Germans who convert to Judaism immediately assume the stamp of competence and proceed to write essays about Jewish identity. In the spring of 1996 a book was published in Germany whose author's concern was nothing less than "a reconsideration of Jewish identity in Germany." He called to the carpet the whole German "empire of Jewish experts" and complained about the "theatrics of remembrance" these experts had staged since 1945: "The Jewish Community and its German Invention." He got so worked up about the "invention" of the Jewish community in Germany that he felt compelled to share with his readers the fact that he was himself an "invented" Jew: Born in 1944 in the Allgau, he'd converted to Judaism in order to dedicate himself to the lifelong service of preserving Jewish identity—a task much too formidable to be left to Jews who were born that way.

The Germanization of the Holocaust turns a historical slaughterhouse into a romper room for a healthy sense of self-esteem: we won't repress it, we aren't ashamed, and we won't settle the account. All we are saying is: isn't it fantastic, the way we stand by our sins?

Of course, the story does have its benefits. Contrary to popular misconception, Germans are not ignorant of their recent history. Surveys confirm that they are well-informed about the period between 1933 and 1945. The German media can be charged with any number of things, but they can't be accused of shying away from a treatment of history, above all that of the Third Reich and the Holocaust. The further the Third Reich recedes into history, the more jobs it creates. Hordes of historians, scholars, and researchers dissect and analyze the interstices of every last detail, however marginal it may seem. Scores of educators, journalists, and artists pick up the fragments, put them in place, and market them as curricula, articles, and works of art. You could say that, fifty years after its demise, the Third Reich has become a mammoth welfare-to-work program that translates into profit for countless small-business contractors. Examples are not only illustrative, they are entertaining.

Since 1988, a citizen's initiative in Berlin, consisting of luminaries led by the journalist Lea Rosh, has been pushing for the construction of a central memorial to the Jews murdered in Europe. After the German government agreed to set aside a twenty-thousand-square-meter plot of land in Berlin's city center, between the Brandenburg Gate and Potsdamer Square, a competition was announced in 1994 in which about two thousand sculptures and architects participated; 528 models were submitted and presented in a public exhibition. We'll come back to that later. For now, suffice it to say that Germany hasn't seen a more impressive collection of kitsch, banality, and nonsense escalated to the point of absurdity since the 1936 Olympics. Nonetheless, this plethora of pathological self-portrayal was telling. Not only did it make clear the impossibility of responding to the Holocaust with a memorial, it also demonstrated, above all, the degree of long-term damage the Holocaust has wrought on the collective German psyche. The menagerie of madness and melancholy, good intentions and bad inventions was simply overwhelming.

At the opening of the exhibition, the jury's foreman, Professor Walter Jens, decreed that a monument should be erected in Berlin to "keep the community of the dead, denied of all dignity and executed, alive." A feat no one had ever accomplished before.

Of the 528 models submitted, seventeen made it to the finals. Since the jury couldn't reach a consensus, two first prizes were awarded. After further deliberations, they decided which of the concepts should actually take shape: a gray cement slab, about one hundred square meters, weighing in at twenty-five thousand tons, and protruding at an angle from the ground would be erected on which the names of the murdered Jews would be engraved over time–after the unveiling, as a "work in progress," so to speak. This, according to Lea Rosh, would "personalize the fate" of the victims; the point was to "bring back the murdered in naming them by name." She countered objections raised about the football-field-sized monument being a testament to German megalomania, saying that the Holocaust was a crime of monolithic proportion and must thus be memorialized by a monument commensurate with its magnitude. An argument that's not entirely wrong, but not quite right either. Just how big would a monument have to be to be commensurate with the enormity of the Holocaust? Is ten thousand square meters sufficient? Or would it take perhaps a million? How about plastering the whole city of Berlin in a concrete slab?

But there was no room for such questions in the euphoric atmosphere in reaction to the news that Berlin would at long last have its very own Holocaust memorial. Only one attentive citizen in the city of Berlin expressed cause for concern in a letter to the editor, pointing out that organizers and participants had "either still failed to comprehend the extent of the genocide of the Jews or obviously couldn't add" because, according to this Berliner, if every name were to be engraved in a twenty-five-by-four-centimeter space, then the slab would have to be 245 by 245 meters long and encompass sixty thousand square meters–that is, it would have to be six times the size of the proposed project. Moreover, if you calculated an hour's work per name, it would take a hundred engravers thirty years to finish the job.

It seemed then, in the summer of 1995, that all systems were go. The slab would cost between twenty and thirty million marks, the federal government and the state of Berlin would underwrite the project, but the bulk of the budget would be subsidized by donations generated through fundraising efforts.

Then something unexpected happened. The chancellor, who had thus far refrained from comment, addressed the issue. He said: No, we don't want a monument of this nature and thus brought the entire project to a standstill by writ of *habeas harumphus.* It was as though, at the last minute, the mayor had cancelled a party that everyone had been anticipating. How can he do this, project backers wondered, when we were just about to begin construction? The commissioner of cultural affairs in Berlin was worried about Germany's standing in the eyes of the international community if the memorial wasn't built. The jury foreman spoke of a "national scandal." Lea Rosh said that her greatest sympathy lies with the dead Jews who would have to wait even longer for their memorial.

Chancellor Kohl justified his decision by saying he considered the prize-winning concept "inappropriately monumental," and he called for a renewed public debate "in order to reach a broad consensus among all parties concerned." Since then, Germany has been engaged in a squabble that confirms the American historian James Young's statement: public debates surrounding the memorial actually constitute the memorial itself. It's a very practical attitude since, on the one hand, it saves a lot of money and, on the other hand, a therapeutic process takes place that no memorial could ever set in motion. Everywhere you go, there are debates, forums, and symposia on the role of public art.

At one such debate, the chairman of the Christian Democratic party in the Berlin Parliament conceded that the planned memorial had involved a "typical political compromise." Policymakers were no longer free to make decisions; no one had dared object to the memorial. Even the historical commission within the Social Democrats' leadership suddenly voiced disapproval for the memorial, which was particularly surprising since, up until then, no one even knew the Social Democrats *had* a historical commission. SPD representative Peter Conradi, who'd also kept silent prior to the chancellor's nay-say, explained: "We need a new debate, a new location, and a new competition." According to Conradi, it was entirely inappropriate that negotiations for a national Holocaust memorial should take place "behind closed doors." The well-known Austrian artist Alfred Hrdlicka hadn't participated in the competition and derided it as an "idiotic" endeavor, recommending instead that "lawn jockeys with Hassidic hairdos" be placed in gardens across the country as a "symbol of German-Jewish reconciliation." When the Jewish Council proclaimed that Germany couldn't afford to be without a monument of this nature, and the SPD faction in the Bundestag demanded that the Parliament be informed of plans to erect the Holocaust memorial, an editor for the arts and leisure section of a Berlin newspaper reminded his readers that the whole city of Berlin had long been a "site of public memory" and, with its forty-odd minor memorial sites, was sufficiently equipped. In other newspapers another expert suggested putting an end to the whole debate, which in turn inspired additional experts to contradict him. So the debate ultimately continued.

A whole cadre of self-proclaimed experts are stepping up to the plate to have their say on why the monument should or should not be built, why it needs to be as big as it is or why it can't be big enough. In what resembles a small-town "disco-dance-line" party, there is no standard of minimal competence required for participation. A statement made by Lothar de Maizière, the last prime minister of the GDR (IM Czerny) stands out in this regard: it would be better to depict fate by collective example than to list the names of millions of victims. Stefan Zweig is said to have died of a broken heart in exile. . . . Meanwhile, Potsdamer Professor Julius H. Schoeps threatens to invoke personal privacy laws and obtain an interim injunction in the event that the names of his relatives are to be engraved in the slab.

Discussions surrounding the Holocaust memorial assume the same degree of solemnity that characterized the planning and execution of the Holocaust itself. This time the only difference is that it involves a public spectacle in which everyone is an able and all-too-willing participant–it represents nothing less than the belated Germanization of the Holocaust. The unfortunate thing is that a few certified experts on the subject of dead Jews are absent from this lively debate. The chief senior public prosecutor Helmut Münzberg, for example, who conducted investigations against SS Obersturmführer Arnold Strippel for serial murder: at Strippel's behest, twenty Jewish children who'd been used in medical experiments in the KZ Neuengamme were hung in a Hamburg school just prior to the war's end. In 1967, Münzberg stayed the preliminary proceedings against the former SS officer who died prematurely and unexposed in 1994, arguing that the murder of the children was "insufficiently cruel and unusual" since the children "had not suffered any damages beyond the loss of their lives."

What a brilliant idea! Perhaps we should invite chief senior public prosecutor Münzberg as a guest of honor at the groundbreaking ceremony for the Holocaust memorial? And wouldn't it be an even brighter idea to chisel the following sentence into the monumental tombstone slab: "In memory of the dead Jews who suffered nothing cruel and unusual beyond the loss of their lives!" Not a single statement in the German postwar litany is better suited to conjoining the failure to pursue the perpetrators with the desire for self-conferred absolution.

Unfortunately, one has to assume that the monument–despite all the assurances to the contrary–will not be built. Because, in the meantime, a certain substitute–at once convenient and cost-effective–has been generated.

In May 1995, while visiting Israel, Bundestag President Rita Süssmuth announced the pending establishment of a national Holocaust memorial day. They had their sights set on January 27, the day Auschwitz was liberated *nota bene* by the Soviet army. Shortly thereafter, the presidents of the provincial ministries approved the proposal, and January 27 was declared National Holocaust Memorial Day. But what was actually to be commemorated remained unclear: "Victims of Tyranny under National Socialism" or "Victims of National-

Socialist Tyranny." It was a minor but utterly crucial distinction. The former would include remembrance of the German expatriates and victims of Allied bombardments, the latter only the immediate victims of Nazis, that is, Jews, Gypsies, homosexuals, and so on. In this way, everyone who felt victimized was to be afforded the opportunity of participating in the commemorations.

The celebration for "Victims of National Socialism"–the lapidary catch-all phrase that was finally agreed upon–would furthermore have to be pushed forward from the twenty-seventh to the nineteenth. Not only did January 27 fall on a Saturday in the year 1996, which would have prevented Jewish guests from participating in official events, German President Herzog had long since slated a trip to Uganda that he did not want to cancel, reschedule, or interrupt. So the Bundestags president delivered a speech to the Bundestag on January 19, elaborating on the meaning of the national holiday: "Remembrance cannot relent because without memory, neither can evil be overcome, nor lessons gleaned for the future." Just before departing for Africa to edify the citizens of Uganda with the benefits of democracy, he said that at least once a year, German citizens should "reflect on what happened and above all, on the conclusions to be drawn from the event." Bundestags President Rita Süssmuth explained that the national holiday should build a "fortress against forgetting" and act as a "thorn in the side of our consciousness." Bavarian Ministry President Stoiber announced, in a sensational news flash, that tremendous crimes had been committed in "the name of Germany," that is to say, on Germany's account but not necessarily by Germans. Claudia Nolte, minister of youth, challenged the country's young people to seek out and speak with survivors. SPD Chairman Oskar Lafontaine said that January 27 "should always serve as a critical point of reference for us Germans to strike a balance with regard to the way we deal with the period of Nazi dictatorship." Throughout the Republic, commemorative celebrations took place in which participants articulated their aversion to Nazi crimes and solemnly vowed to never allow a Holocaust to happen again. And, just to be sure no mistakes would be made, prominent experts on the proper protocol for this type of memorial were asked how a day like this would have to be staged: the left-wing Berlin daily, *die taz,* interviewed the Israeli author Uri Avnery on the subject of "Routine and Remembrance," while the more mainstream *Tagesspiegel* spoke with South African Bishop Desmond Tutu about reconciliation between perpetrators and victims, and the liberal *Frankfurter Rundschau* printed a conversation with Nobel Prize–winning author Elie Wiesel, who spoke in terms of a "significant change of course": "For so many years, the people of Germany have sought to forget. They set aside what happened here, ignored it, looked the other way. Now, confronting the past has become paramount."

Not even Elie Wiesel, who is said to have coined the term *holocaust*, asked how, more or less overnight, Germans fell from one extreme to the other, with national rhetoric changing from a lukewarm "Let this crap rest in peace!" to a flamboyant "We can't get enough of it!" He was content with the change in course. Adherents to the theory of the German Volksseele may seek an explanation for the phenomenon in the very essence of the German Volk, which displays a marked tendency toward manic-depressive behavior. Even Winston Churchill said that you either had the Germans at your throat or at your feet. This sort of pop-psych analysis might be nice, but it can't suffice. Why is it that for so long the Germans wanted nothing to do with the Holocaust, ignored it, and set it aside? And why is an entire nation of contenders suddenly goose-stepping in a Memorial Marathon?

It's not only a matter of the central Holocaust memorial in Berlin and the Holocaust memorial holiday. In Berlin, a half-dozen memorials have been erected in memory of the book burnings and the murder and deportation of the Jews. An exhibition of photographs from the German concentration camps, titled "Dead Silent," first opened in Berlin, then was put on display in other cities. An exhibition with the theme "After Auschwitz," in which twenty artists from twelve countries participated, was brought to Potsdam. Its centerpiece was a stereoscopic installation consisting of suitcases and titled "Wailing Wall." One of the suitcases came from the court exhibit chambers of Auschwitz. The German Historical Museum in Berlin acquisitioned a piece by the Polish sculptor Miecyzslaw Stobierski–a miniature replica of Crematoria II at Auschwitz-Birkenau on a scale of 1:15 with three thousand plaster figurines. At the site of Prinz-Albert-Gelände, where the Gestapo headquarters were located, construction is currently under way for an exhibition, documentation, and meeting center–"A Place for Thinking and Learning."

But it's not only in the nation's capital that something's afoot; the backwoods are abuzz as well. In Frankfurt, lavish efforts were invested in the erection of an "Educational and Documentary Center for the Holocaust." In Darmstadt, they're working on a project to compile a comprehensive register of all the inmates of the camp at Auschwitz. The Evangelical Academy in Loccum hosted a conference for experts on "Memorials at the Site of Former Concentration Camps." Just outside Berlin, in Wandlitz, where there are de facto no Jews, there is talk of creating a "Jewish Cultural and Neighborhood Center." The poet and folk singer Wolf Bierman was invited to the Bundestag in Bonn to present before the representatives in the Hallowed Halls "The Song of the Extirpated Jewish People" by Yitzhak Katzenelson, a Jewish poet murdered by the Nazis.

Isn't the all-pervasive memory of the Holocaust just fantastic? You can feel it everywhere–in politics, in culture, even in the way we spend our free time.

You have to admit that the Germans treat the subject of their past with utmost sensitivity. And the further this past recedes into the distance, the more sensitive its treatment. At issue is no longer the Holocaust and its victims; it has since become an exercise dubbed "The Pedagogy of Transmission." An interview with a preeminent Holocaust scholar on the stress and psychological problems ensuing from such engagement recently appeared in the *taz*. It may have been all over for the Jews in 1945, but Holocaust scholars are still suffering the aftereffects today. It won't be long before *they* become the ones who suffer the burden of history. Not only do yesterday's catastrophes provide the stuff of tomorrow's doctoral dissertations, the Holocaust has been a veritable boon to German history. It's hard to imagine what would have happened had the British or French staged the Holocaust. But this way, we are afforded the opportunity of witnessing on an almost daily basis the extent to which the Holocaust determines the behavior of people in Germany.

The German airline Eurowings traded in the NS identification code for another from an Australian airline, EW, because NS "was laden with too many negative associations." Two of the barracks destroyed by arson at the former KZ Sachsenhausen are being restored to their original condition, which is utterly absurd, but which satisfied the need for morbid authenticity, just like the Auschwitz suitcase on exhibit in the art show in Potsdam. The German federal government provides subsidies in the amount of a couple of million marks a year for the ongoing restoration project at the Auschwitz camp, which is only logical: after all, the Germans are the ones who built the camp, so they should be the ones to cover maintenance costs.

My question is: Do all these maneuvers and rituals surrounding the Holocaust have any impact on the conduct toward living human beings, Jews and non-Jews alike? What, in the final analysis, is the effect of the "fortress against forgetting"? And how does the "thorn in our consciousness" work when what is at stake is not bemoaning the dead who've been denied a memorial but rather helping people who can't help themselves?

While symbolic resistance to Hitler and the Nazis is fortified day by day, indifference toward the few remaining victims of Nazi terror still alive declines in direct proportion.

Since 1986 negotiations have continued regarding the establishment of a foundation whose budget would provide "compensation" to victims who weren't included in previous reparation agreements: homosexuals, Gypsies, and people subjected to forced sterilization. The politicians are obviously hoping the problem will take care of itself.

Similarly, Nazi courts sentenced over a hundred thousand conscientious objectors and deserters to years of hard labor. Over twenty thousand were executed. These verdicts have never been overturned, and in the eyes of the law, the deserters are still convicted criminals. Three hundred of them are still alive and fighting for repatriation. In vain! The majority of representatives in the Bundestag refuses to pass a law to restore rights and honor to the deserters. Repatriating the deserters, so they say, would be a dishonor to those soldiers in the Wehrmacht "who fought to the end." That's what the "fortress against forgetting" looks like when it's put into practice!

Resistance against Hitler is always brought to the fore whenever the other, new and improved Germany must be called upon for reasons of national PR. But the reality of the situation is altogether different. Even the Christian resistance fighter Dietrich Bonhoeffer, who was sentenced to death and executed by an SS court on April 9, 1945, hasn't yet been rehabilitated, even though he is paraded before school children to set a moral example. In 1956, the federal Supreme Court ruled that Bonhoeffer's death sentence had to be upheld because it was a matter of the state's "right of self-determination," one that cannot be "patently denied even the National-Socialist state."

Against this backdrop, the solemn testimonials now being issued by German politicians in honor of Holocaust victims cannot be regarded as anything but cynical maneuvers with the sole intent of making the authors of these spectacles feel good and improve Germany's public image. The Germanization of the Holocaust has been a successful experiment in transforming historical liability into moral capital–the interest on the investment alone far exceeds what has been paid out to victims in "compensation."

*Translated by Lilian M. Friedberg*

# 13

## PROBLEM, SHOCK, AND TRAUMA

When you order food at an Israeli locale—let's say an appetizer, soup, or an entreé—the waiter will not respond to your request with a "Thank you," "Will that be all?" or "Do you want rice or potatoes?" No, he instead raises his eyebrows and ends the event with two words: *Ejn baja*, "no problem." You hear the same two words when you ask a gas-station attendant to fill up the tank, or if you want to exchange money at the bank or send a fax from the post office: *Ejn baja*, "no problem."

Of course there is no shortage of groceries in the country, you don't need a ration card to get gas, and the postal employee who at one time only sold stamps can now provide fax service. The ubiquitous assurance that this or that is no problem comes from the subconscious presumption to the contrary. If all things belonged in their right place, it would have to be a problem to get a meal, fill up the tank, or change traveler's checks. But only when he is faced with a problem to solve can an Israeli prove to himself and the world that he is capable of mastering life's little vices. You see, an existence without enormous difficulties to overcome, without obstacles to be surmounted, would–after two thousand years of fighting for survival–be no fitting form of existence.

*Jesch lanu baja*, "there we have a problem," is the standard mark of a real Israeli, regardless of whether the fan belt blew on the Autobahn, or his wife left him for his best friend, or even if the roof was whisked away. The three words are intoned precisely, as if their articulation reconstituted the natural order of things. The Italian sings, the Frenchman drinks, the German works, and the Israeli has a problem to solve. And when temporarily no problem avails itself because there are no bus drivers on strike, all the teachers are teaching, and Sara Netanyahu has paid her hairdresser and the nanny, then it takes a couple of days until a problem is created for the nation to work out. Either the religious parties threaten to leave a coalition when they receive no more state subsidies for their institutions or the Orthodox lead themselves to be slaughtered by the police because somewhere in the country a street is to be built over an old grave site. A surefire source of conflict that keeps cropping up is asking the question: "Who's a Jew?" Someone born of a Jewish mother? Someone who knows precisely where the best bargains are? Or is it perhaps enough to own an apartment in Jerusalem or to fly from New York to Tel Aviv with El Al instead of with a major airline?

However, the more personal the encounter with the problem, the more fun it becomes. A Tel Aviv stock market crash is nothing compared to missing a bus that pulls away right before your nose. In such a situation the authentic Israeli does not say *Jesch li baja*, "I have a problem," but instead *kibalti schock*, "I was shocked." And if, as a result of the bus having pulled away right under his nose, he missed the start of the news broadcast at home, he takes it one step further and says: *Jesch li trauma*, "I was traumatized." The Israeli, then, tends toward subtle exaggerations to describe his momentary plight.

Amazingly, the opposite is also applicable. As a collective, Israelis reveal their mark of distinction through a composure that one finds nowhere else in the world. In no other country would people run around for weeks with gas masks prepared for attack; in no other country would people sit night after night in protective bunkers, all knowing that if it really came down to it, they would offer no protection. It appears as if clear and present danger has a calming, disciplined effect, whereas the everyday situations that require composure and thoughtfulness are way too much for them to handle.

"The war is imminent, we are becoming nice to each other," was announced on the front page of the *Jerusalem Post* immediately before the outbreak of the Gulf War. And when a post office has to be evacuated because someone left a shopping bag lying around that could contain a bomb, everyone waits quietly and patiently outside the door until the bomb squad has been called in to examine the bag and "de-fuse" it. However, the calm and composure is out the window soon after the contents prove to be harmless: everyone fights to regain the same place in line he'd had before the alarm. There's hell to pay for anyone who dares cut ahead in line: he becomes the target for the full brunt of rage that should have been directed at the suspected terrorists.

The actual war in Israel takes place on the street. Month for month more people are killed in car accidents than are murdered by Arab terrorists. The one cause of death is as senseless as the other, but drivers, unlike terrorists, can at least count on a modicum of lenience. *Jesch lanu baja?* "Do we have a problem?" Not necessarily, because the Israeli driver considers himself among the best in the world. This spurious assumption would be only half as bad if he didn't do everything in his power to prove it, which only leads to more fatalities. Of course, there is a reason for this tremendous gap between praxis and self-appraisal. No one whose parents and grandparents were still on a wagon traveling through the Ukraine or riding atop a donkey through Casablanca can develop a reasonable relationship with a machine under his rear. Civilization needs time to establish itself. Even the British had to practice for a long time for pretence to become flesh and blood.

So it is that each Israeli who can keep a steady grip on the steering wheel views every disruption of traffic that compels him to make a detour not as something completely normal but as a personal injury, a blow to his honor. Mustering the last reserves of his remaining energy, he barely manages to threaten another driver with a fight for causing the situation and warns him to think twice about coming too close to him. There is something similar in other societies, but in no other civilized country will bad manners be defended so vehemently as a basic civil right as in Israel. Let's say a man attempts to place a call from a public telephone. Perhaps the telephone is broken, a situation that can occur anywhere. Yet a man takes it personally, as if the last caller had broken it intentionally, just to annoy him. In his anger, he slams the receiver as though he wanted to exorcise a Dybuk from the phone box. "What are you doing there?" a person asks while passing by, "You trying to break the thing?" Now the first man has finally found someone against whom he can really let out his frustrations. "What's it to you? Is it your telephone? Did you pay for it?" he growls. "Don't you have anything better to do than run around here and give me advice?" That would be enough anywhere to clear up the situation, but he must conclude his tirade with, "Go home and fuck yourself, you son of a bitch!" And with that, everyone is satisfied. The first man was shocked because he couldn't use the telephone, the second traumatized because he was insulted. And both "have a problem," *jesch lanu baja.* Blessed is the Lord, for we are in fact *am echad,* "a people of brothers and sisters" who love one another and look out for one another.

The Israelis describe their own collective condition as a form of "hysterical composure," tending at times more towards hysteria and at others towards composure. As the songstress Naomi Shemer sings: "One day festival, one day carnival." It only took twenty-four hours for normalcy to return to the area after an attack in the Ben-Yehuda Street in Jerusalem. There, in early September 1997, four pedestrians were killed and dozens more injured. While the "merciful men" from the "Hevra kadischa" were still busy scraping minute body parts from the windows of houses, the Café Atara, Café Chagall, and Café Rimon had already set up shop again, open for business with customers waiting to be served. *Ejn baja,* "no problem," you have to prove to yourself and the whole world that there is only one way to fight terrorism: proceed, business as usual, as if nothing had happened.

Israelis have learned to live with catastrophes. There are water shortages in summer, flooding in winter, and internal incompetence and external terrorist threats year-round. "Never a dull moment!" as the native Israeli boasts to a tourist. Yet, other mottos would fit better. For one: "Always more of the same," because the stories, affairs, and scandals repeat themselves, as if in an endless loop. And, in the interim, proletarian revolution is played. The labor unions call a general strike, and the country is paralyzed; thousands of tourists get stranded at the airport, and no one feels responsible for their plight. On TV, there were no weather predictions because the human groundhogs are organized by labor.

Viewed from a certain distance, such compulsion is fascinating. Israel produces more news than it can consume on its own. That's why the German television broadcasts the Knesset elections live, as if the Jewish state were a Bundesland on the southern fringes of the Republic. German daily news reports have even been known to run as their lead story the findings of a government session led by Benjamin Netanyahu in a sixteen-to-zero vote to postpone a decision concerning the second phase of the clearing of the West Bank, as if nothing else important happened in the world.

Whoever has not been raised in Israel will probably never understand when a problem really is one. In Tel Aviv even the garbage men strike. After two weeks, everyone is living on top of a huge garbage heap, while stores and restaurants close because the shit is piled a meter high on the sidewalk. People wear gas masks in order to breathe. The city becomes a haven for rats. No problem, the mayor will figure it out! At the same time, a committee comprised of seven Supreme Court judges is installed to decide whether unpaid parking tickets should fall under the statute of limitations after three years or ten—finally, a problem calling to the heavens to be resolved.

And if one day the Messiah should in fact appear, the Iraelis will still be of divided opinion. *Ejn baja*, some will say: "we will manage," *Jesch lanu bana*, the others: "Oh, just what we needed."

*Translated by Christopher Brummer*

14

## YOU'RE NOT DEAD

## TILL YOU GIVE UP THE FIGHT

Andy Warhol once said everyone is entitled to fifteen minutes of fame. But in
a country like Israel, just one minute will suffice. A mini-report on Channel
Two of the Israeli TV made Shoshana ("the Rose") Blechmann the heroine of
the militant Right. She had composed a song for Baruch Goldstein that began
with the same two words as prayers to the Almighty: *Baruch ata . . .* "Blessed
be thy name! Doctor Goldstein." For her, this physician from Kirjat Arba who
killed twenty-nine Palestinians at prayer was "not a murderer, but rather a
saint and a soldier, like David fighting Goliath back in olden days."

Shoshana Blechmann, born in 1929 in Montevideo, sits now in the Tnuva-
Café on the Ben Gurion Boulevard in Tel Aviv. For breakfast she's just wolfed
down a large tuna salad. She wipes the bowl clean with a piece of bread, de-
vours the last morsels, and orders a latté to wash it all down. When she speaks,
she scoots up to the table and boldly plops her megatits on its top, her feet all
the while swinging above the floor. If Adam, Hoss, and Little Joe had had a
"Ma" alongside their "Pa," she'd likely have been named "Rose" and looked

like Shoshana: small, but strong. And no one on the Ponderosa would have dared get in her way.

Shoshana's mother emigrated from Bessarabien to South America, her father from Transylvania. At home, Yiddish, "an awful dialect," was spoken; already as a child she had dreamt "of just being in Israel." In 1963 she moved with her new husband Merel to the country of her dreams, learned Hebrew, and worked as a music teacher in various schools. It was, however, first with her retirement in 1994 that the natural-born renegade could become what she always wanted to be–a hot-headed rebel.

"I've wanted a revolver for a long time," she enunciated as if she were talking about a car with automatic transmission, but for the longest time "those idiots" in the Ministry of the Interior didn't want to give her a gun permit. "They told me: 'You do not have the right credentials.' And I replied: 'I'll show you what my credentials are!'" With her only savings she bought a small house for forty-five thousand dollars in Eli, an isolated settlement north of Jerusalem between Ramallah and Nablus. There she immediately received a gun permit, for whoever lives in "Judea and Samaria" must of course be able to defend herself in case of emergency.

Shoshana found herself "a small Smith and Wesson" and learned to shoot. Ever since, she's felt "more secure"–particularly when she drives once a week from Eli to Tel Aviv, where she still has her old apartment. She stays for a day or two in the city, then drives back to Eli where she finds her boxer, Rex, and her son, Ruben, awaiting anxiously. "That's an adventure: I drive back and forth, and it never gets boring." Besides that, "the quality of life in Eli is much better, like in Switzerland. . . . It's a whole new world," and even the "people are different–they don't run around in such a rush like in Tel Aviv."

Nonetheless, Shoshana's idols are no slackers but rather heroes like Ze'ev Yabotinsky, who, in the twenties and thirties, was the leader of right-wing Zionists and a mentor to Menachem Begin. And then there's Josef Trumpeldor, who died in 1920 while defending a Jewish settlement against Arab attackers. His last words were, "it feels good to die for our country."

But she can only revile and scoff at today's Israelis. "Just look at these Jews. In their own country they behave like they do in the Diaspora. They get down on their knees, begging for freedom, and for that get a kick in the ass. You do not get peace on your knees. There is no 'people' here, only sheep." What Jews lack above all else is "honor and self-discipline." There is no people in the world that would stand idly by and allow "someone to burn their flag before their very eyes." "My people is that struggling Jewish people, not the Jews who scuttle around on their knees. There's no such thing as life without a struggle. Life itself–from birth to death–is a struggle. If you're not fighting to survive, you're not even alive." In Spanish there's a clever saying: you're not dead till you give up the fight.

The Israelis have "no perseverance and sense," they would only "run after pleasure and let the Arabs do the work." "That's no good, if you haven't worked the soil with your own hands, it's not yours to own. These idiots do not understand this." Besides that they are "sick" and "masochists"; they love to "piss and moan" without ever lifting a finger. "The few non-idiots there are in this country don't stand a chance against the idiot majority!" "There's not a soul around who could help you start a revolution." And even worse are the people from "Schalom achscaw!" (Peace now!)–even "worse than the Arabs." No, she doesn't hate the Arabs, they're in a terrible situation, after all: "Whoever wants to be Israel's friend will kill the Hamas and we'll kill anyone who doesn't want to be friends with Israel."

Just like Baruch Goldstein, for whom Shoshana composed "The Song of the Physician"? He was a good Jew, a doctor, and a saint. He knew the Arabs were going to attack the Jews, and he simply struck first. He did what we all must do: "make a pre-emptive strike."

Shoshana can't say how Goldstein knew what the Arabs were planning, she heard it from others who must have known that "in the area weapons were hidden to massacre the Jews."

Yet the Israeli media would never report that; instead they speculate "whether he had a difficult childhood." "I identify with Dr. Goldstein's actions. Others just talked, he acted."

Was it worth dying for?

"Who said: Life is not the most valuable good? Schiller? Goethe? Trumpeldor?"

No matter who it was, Shoshana Blechman was amazed by and admired "Doctor Goldstein" as if he had saved twenty-nine lives before dying, as opposed to having destroyed them. She herself was supposedly "too old" to do anything like that, but if one day she were told she had "cancer and only had a month to live" then, who knows. . . . She plops her megatits on the table, leans forward, and says: "I would have the necessary will for it. If I have to die, then not like a sheep." When it's all said and done, she would like to look herself in the mirror and say: "Shoshana, you should be proud of yourself, you did what you thought was right!"

A little while ago a leftist Knesset member warned people about her, describing her as "a threat"–which pleased her. Later, Baruch Goldstein's father and mother called to thank her for the song. "You must be very proud of your son," she said to the parents.

"I'm fine, I'm happy, I lack nothing. I can do as I please; that is my luxury."

Shoshana gets up every day at six to take a walk with Rex. She gives private music lessons, grows tomatoes in her garden, and reads detective novels in Spanish. The "hot-headed rebel" packs her Smith and Wesson revolver once a month when she goes to target practice in Tel Aviv. She would never move out of Eli, even if the settlement came under Palestinian occupation. "I'm staying here; here I have a reason to fight."

For the next Purim festival, which coincided with the fourth day of mourning for Baruch Goldstein, she prepared in "Moadon," Eli's Kulturklub, a "Tutti-frutti-song night in all languages." There the "Song of the Doctor" will be presented: "Blessed be thy name, Doctor Baruch Goldstein, you who have sanctified the name of God in Machpela. . . ."

*Translated by Christopher Brummer*

# 15

## TAGAR AND THE

## TEEPEE FAMILY

Tagar is a German shepherd dog with a pedigree "reaching as far back as Hitler." Loosely translated, his name means "Challenger" and was inspired by a poem by Wladimir Yabotinsky, the leader of the right-wing extremist Zionists in the twenties and thirties. But unlike his famous cousin, Blondie, Tagar won't allow you to pet him. He barks, bares his teeth, and immediately shrinks back as soon as he is approached.

"We bought him from a Russian family," says June Leavitt while making two cups of tea from one tea bag.

If Tagar could talk and not just bark, he'd probably request permission for his immediate return to Russia, because the beast's life is like living in a doghouse. There aren't any public parks fit for a dog in Kirjat Arba and, when his mistress takes him out for a walk, the two of them stroll along the three-and-a-half-foot-high barbed-wire fence separating the Jewish Kirjat Arba from the Arab Hebron. Aside from that, Tagar lives with two adults and five children in a four-room, eighty-square-meter apartment that looks more like a homeless shelter that's never been cleaned. A bare light bulb dangling from its fixture sheds just enough light to outline the contours of the miserable conditions. Beneath the ceiling in the hallway connecting the three minibedrooms there is laundry hanging that never seems to dry; the shelves are laden with tomes bound in imitation leather, the Bible and other historical masterpieces. Barbells of varying size are strewn beneath the convertible couch.

"My husband's been lifting weights," says June Leavitt, as though she were trying to allay any suspicion of wasting her time on bodybuilding. June Leavitt, after all, is an author—born in New York in 1950 under the maiden name June Oppenheimer. She writes books. Her *Diary of a Jewish Settler* was published in France and in Germany. The novel *Falling Star*, about an orthodox Jewish girl from Brooklyn who drives her dad to distraction by falling in love with a Gentile, is slated to appear in 1998 in the United States. June speaks Hebrew with a pronounced American accent and dresses like an aging flower child whose closet never made it past the hippie era. At the University of Wisconsin at Madison, where she'd fled New York after high school, she studied a "steady diet of the sixties, Buddhism included," and was conferred a B.A. in English. In 1979, she moved to Israel with her husband Frank and lived in the settlement of Atzmona in the Sinai until Sinai was returned to Egypt in April 1982. After a couple of weeks on the Gaza Strip, she took refuge in Beit Romano, an old Jewish establishment in the middle of Hebron.

Since 1984, the Leavitt family has been living in Kirjat Arba. Frank lectures on "Medicine and Ethics" four times a week at the University of Beer Sheva. June gives private English lessons in Jerusalem and offers seminars in self-discovery for adults. After years of searching, she's finally concluded her own lifelong quest for her "inner self," and she has found it in a world "where the reality submerged beneath the surface" is crucial, where "not politics but spirituality is what matters." That's why the Leavitt family does not own a television but Janis Joplin and Cat Stevens albums instead.

The quest for her own identity began when June was twenty-four and had a "vision": "Indians, a teepee-tent, a life in tune with nature in the middle of the forest." An acquaintance had told her about some people in Vermont "who still lived in teepees." She went to Vermont, but instead of finding Indians living there in teepees, she met "a long-haired man with a beard and sparkling blue eyes"—Frank. A week later, they were to spend a "moonless night" together, "when he was suddenly overcome by his long-since-forgotten Jewish heritage." Frank owned a plot of land on which the two of them built "a Mongolian style cabin" and lived without electricity or gas, only spring water and a kerosene lantern that provided enough light for them to read "books on gardening." They cooked on a grill. June worked on illustrations for a children's book. Frank learned to play the recorder from a Greek Orthodox priest. "We lived in perfect harmony with nature and were healthy and strong."

Two years passed like this until one day a copy of the Old Testament fell into June's hands, and she said to Frank: "Honey, I'd really like to get to know the ancient Jews." Frank, too, felt the pangs of "hunger for a spiritual home" and wondered whether he should be baptized and become a Christian. He left it to chance and flipped a coin: heads, he'd "take holy communion"; tails, he'd "seek out a Rabbi." Frank got lucky. "The flip of the coin was in favor of Judaism."

June and Frank abandoned the cabin and moved to Crown Heights in Brooklyn; he visited a Lubawitscher-Yeshiva for "Jewish men with limited knowledge of Judaism"; she attended a seminar for women designed to "bring her closer to Judaism." But life in the city made her "sick." After a couple of months, they moved back to the land, started a compost heap, and raised chickens and sheep. This time, though, everything was kosher, and they paid careful attention to the "relationship between the commandments and nature."

Cut. June Leavitt's *Diary of a Jewish Settler* begins with a winter storm in February 1992. She's been living in Kirjat Arba for eight years and asks herself: "Why is this miserable life my fate . . . ?" In the beginning, it was "all just a big adventure," but suddenly it occurs to her that she's "living in a cramped apartment in the middle of a settlement fenced in by barbed wire," "conditions that only exist in the Third World." On the other side of the encampment, there is nothing but hostile Arabs, and in her own building "neighbors who can hear your every move." The walls are so thin "you can hear your neighbor taking a piss." June wonders "if I'm not rather like an old plant that's been repotted in inhospitable soil?" An inner voice poses unpleasant questions: "Was our Earth really worth the loss of blood and lives our people sacrificed for it?" In Hebron "the price for mystic nationalism is paid in human lives." In Kirjat Arba "concentrated religious sanctimony" prevails. The mandatory peaceful respite of the Sabbath is a "terrible burden." June is always sick, and there isn't a doctor who can "figure out what's wrong." By now, she's got five kids and feels old and weary. "This country, that much is certain, takes its toll on its own population."

But, now and again, there are good moments. June and Frank take their kids to Ein Gedi on the Dead Sea. "People come here from all over the world. We literally thirst for the chance to meet people who aren't Jews for a change."

They meet two women from Switzerland, Erica and Elisabeth, "Victims of feminism and free love," whose husbands have left them. They've come to Israel to "make sense of their lives." Back in Kirjat Arba, her daily routine gets the better of June. She has trouble sleeping nights, is in a constant state of poor

health, and fights "the forces dragging us to the grave." Winter only exacer-
bates her fits of depression. "The apartments are small, poorly insulated, and
without central heating. There's a build-up of black, damp mold on the walls."
Seven people living "in a prison with just four rooms." A neighbor, Miriam
Goldstein, the wife of Baruch Goldstein, says, "she, too, is losing ground. She
feels like she ages five years for every year she spends here."

June develops gall stones and is thankful "that it's no worse than that!" When
her entire immune system collapses, she notes: "Kirjat Arba is killing me!"
Others actually do die: "Friends and acquaintances are being murdered" on
the way to Kirjat Arba or while visiting Hebron. Frank is critically injured at
the wheel when he's hit by a stone thrown by a Palestinian. His son escapes
with his life from a bus hijacking. "We are engaged in a terrible battle. The
price we pay could be our lives."

On February 25, 1994, when Baruch Goldstein massacred worshiping Arabs in the "Cave of the Patriarchs," June's first hope was that "some lunatic
had gone to Hebron, not a member of our settlement." Once it became clear
that the culprit was indeed the beloved pediatrician from Kirjat Arba, she broke
out in tears. But she was not mourning the victims of the bloodbath: "I shed
tears for his widow, Miriam, whom I've known for years, and for his four children." Goldstein's crime, after all, was a break with tradition: "For the past two
thousand years, history has taught us that the Jews are the victims of massacres, never the perpetrators."

Most people in Kirjat Arba consider "Baruch an angel in a man's body, a good
father, a good husband, and a good doctor." They call him "a saint and a sav-
ior." June concedes to "living among a horde of dangerous extremists," yet, at
the same time, she thinks "maybe Baruch Goldstein has done some good,"
because "not a single Jew has been killed since the massacre." Suddenly, she
is struck by an brilliant idea: "If Baruch Goldstein . . . was a modern-day Sam-
son, maybe then one of my sons will become a born-again Moses."

In spite of the many insights it inspires, life in Kirjat Arba is not without long-
term consequences. After the ratification of the Israeli peace accord with Jordan in the summer of 1994, June noted: "This peace brings with it the risk of
internationalizing Israel, the risk of assimilating the Jews among other nations
of the earth, the dissolution and final disappearance of the ancient Jewish
soul. . . . It is precisely the absence of peace with others that has shaped our
personality. . . ."

Her confidence is shaken: "Are we really God's chosen people? Or were the
Arabs perhaps the Chosen Ones?" When a neighbor is arrested by the police
and retained for questioning, allegedly just because he was planning a trip to

the Ukraine where he intended to pray at the grave of Rabbi Nachman, June shrieks in indignation: "People of the world, rise up and fight this crime against humanity, fight this police state that calls itself a democracy, this Israel!"

While visiting Tel Aviv, June and Frank are awestruck by all the "wonderful promenades" and "all these luxury hotels." Frank says, "It won't last. This isn't why the Jews were put on Earth." And he has a vision: "A terrible war" will destroy all this worldly splendor.

Suddenly, life in Kirjat Arba is viewed in an entirely different light, even though seven people have been killed in Palestinian terrorist attacks "on the dangerous streets" in the course of only four months. Nevertheless, Kirjat Arba is "much safer than other places" in the world and in Israel.

"There's almost no crime here. No one locks the doors. Kids can walk home alone at night when they've been out visiting friends and no one needs to worry about them." What is more, "I have the feeling that I'm not alone. These are the days of the New Messiah."

If only the government weren't so stupid! They're "giving up the land! What little space we have left for planting carrots is getting smaller and smaller." The land is being "abused for industrial development," the desert "sacrificed . . . to the construction of an Autobahn."

When a "Jewish woman from Hebron" is kept from shopping at the Arab market by Israeli police, June experiences a sense of déjà vu: "What I'm writing sounds unbelievable. But that's precisely what the people thought when the first reports of the gas chambers in Nazi Germany were made public." And, shortly thereafter, when news is released of the pending surrender of parts of Hebron to the Palestinians, she's overcome by desperation and has only one wish: "To drink fresh spring water, to eat fruit fresh from the tree, and to recuperate from the past fifteen years."

But, two weeks later, she's gotten a grip on herself and is preparing for the future. In spite of it all, "this is the place we call home. This is where our roots are, and that's why we've decided to venture a major investment in our apartment. We've contracted Avner to build us a bathtub."

That could explain a lot of things. Ten years in a house without a bathtub take their toll on more than personal hygiene. Apparently, they affect the mental condition of the house's inhabitants. Of course, in this case, as always, the question arises of what came first, the chicken or the egg? Are certain situations created by certain individuals or do certain situations simply attract certain types of individuals?

The question seems rhetorical, as does the answer. The circular logic of the egg-chicken-egg versus chicken-egg-chicken is at work in Kirjat Arba.

Of course, at the Oktoberfest you run into a different crowd than you would at a Nigel Kennedy open-air concert. It seems equally self-evident that a different kind of exuberance prevails at a Ballermann on the island of Mallorca than at a Wim Wenders party. Seen from that perspective, it's no coincidence that June Leavitt has settled down in Kirjat Arba and not in Zichron Ya'akov or Rosch Pina—historical places in the heart of Israel's interior. Neither Zichron Ya'akov nor Rosch Pina is fenced in barbed wire, and the risk of being killed by a Palestinian terrorist on the way home is much smaller than that of being run over by an Israeli who has overestimated his own driving ability. June Leavitt hasn't moved to Kirjat Arba in spite of the dangers and miserable conditions, but precisely because of them. While the majority of Israelis strive for "corruption" through affluence—in the best sense of the word—June Leavitt embodies the age-old Jewish experience that determined their existence in the ghetto and the Shtetl: Why on earth should life be fun when it can be arduous and exhausting? Thriving is not a Jewish virtue—but striving to survive is.

That is why you find so many people in the settlements who speak in terms of having a special assignment, an ordained duty, or a mission and who have nothing but disdain for the hedonistic citizens of Tel Aviv who would rather spend their days lounging at the beach or in the cafes.

And if you ask them why they feel the need to live in Kirjat Arba—a place that is not only hopelessly desolate, ugly, and run-down but also rather remote and dangerous, then they take recourse to a historical argument intended to function like a time-machine: Was not every settlement in the country once remote? Wasn't the Jewish Tel Aviv once under siege from the Arab Yafo, just like the Jewish Kirjat Arba is now bombarded with stones from the Arab Hebron? The settlements in Judea, Samaria, and Gaza aren't all that lie surrounded by Arab enemy territory, all of Israel is just a tiny island in an Arabian ocean under constant threat of tides and torrents. Life in Kirjat Arba, then, is just like life in the rest of Israel, only a bit more extreme.

The argument isn't wholly spurious. In fact, it has its own inner logic—if you ignore the fact that 1998 is not 1948 and certainly not 1928. The difference is not only that Israel has reached a peace accord with Egypt and Jordan and conducts diplomatic relations with a dozen additional Arab nations. The argument furthermore patently negates any notion of the possibility that the Palestinians may have been equally susceptible to the "corruption" of affluence that has befallen the Israelis.

The same applies to the argument that the settlements are crucial to the security of Israel. Precisely the opposite is true. The army has to invest tremendous resources in guaranteeing the security of the settlements. If it came down to it, June and Frank would not be in a position to defend their newly installed bathtub with their own hands. They'd either be trampled or in need of evacuation, which would only slow down or weaken the Israeli army.

So just what kind of logic is at work behind the madness? Or, to put it another way: What form of madness lurks behind the ostensible logic?

The Holocaust–what else? It is no coincidence that there is hardly a "native" Israeli or Holocaust survivor to be found among the inhabitants of Kirjat Arba and the other settlements. Eljakim Ha'etzni, a native of Kiel, Germany, is the rare and atypical exception. Absolutely nothing can drive anyone who actually experienced the ghetto and the camp to return to similar circumstances. But the American immigrants who've settled in Judea, Samaria, and Gaza are cut from a different cloth. One cannot maintain that the American Jews went overboard in their efforts to help the persecuted Jewish populations in Europe. They didn't even manage to rescue the 930 Jewish passengers on board the St. Louis when it showed up in New York in June 1939. Now, as if to offer symbolic atonement for the forfeitures of the past, they reenact history on a "public playground"–placing themselves in the role of the potential victim. That is why they are so happy to speak in terms of massacres past and pending–of the danger they expose themselves to, of the necessity for resistance–if need be, even against a government that knows not what it does. But there's another twist to the tale: American Jews, whose greatest existential quandary is whether to spend Passover in the Catskills or in Florida, are finally afforded– that is, they now seize–the opportunity to experience that "authentic" Jewish existence they know only from literature and hearsay: life in the ghetto, surrounded by malicious enemies who could at any given time initiate a pogrom. Yes, that's how it must have been for the Cossacks who blazed a trail of blood through the Shtetl, it's just that today they answer to the name of Ahmed, Yassir, and Mahmoud.

But the whole thing only works as longs as it remains virtual reality–that is, as long as the self-fulfilling fantasy of the pogrom never actually goes into effect. So a fatality here and there is accepted as the cost of doing business and is bid farewell with a "Now more than ever!"

Consider Rapheal, for example, June and Frank's neighbor, who one fine day decided to become an Orthodox Jew after he'd spent several years among the "Jews for Jesus." He lost his life in a terrorist attack near Hebron only four months after he'd married Chaja. His widow is convinced that "he would have been proud to have known how many people bowed before his mortal remains . . . paying their respects, to have known how many prominent and well-known rabbis came to mourn his death, this man who, just four months prior, had been a nobody." Well, Raphael may be a somebody now, but somehow he's gotten nothing out of the deal.

And Chaja, pregnant with proud sorrow, has found her "calling": "I am the prophet Deborah. I must learn how to use an Uzi. And I will go to war against the Amalek."

The Amaleks, an Arabic tribe, were the arch enemies of the Jews during biblical times.

Cut. "We're still here," says June, "we've tried to leave several times, but something kept us here." She says it is the "Hebron sickness," a spiritual bond that not everyone feels. "It's more than you can see with the eye."

June speaks of wisdom, spirit vision, and mysticism. "By staying here, we have attained inner maturity, we see more of the light, feel more fortune, and experience more joy." A quiet life is shallow, and there is nothing worse than boredom. And those "who manage to survive all the catastrophes grow beyond themselves."

But isn't daily life in Israel exciting enough in itself? Government crises, corruption scandals, and the constant pursuit of peace?

"Politics and politicians bore me to death," says June, but at the same time, she was happy that Netanyahu took over the government, "even though he's not exactly the greatest Jewish leader," but he at least managed to ensure a greater degree of security. And now she can sense the dawning of a new age. "Something really big is about to emerge, something we can't yet imagine today," and the Jewish people must follow their calling to be a beacon among peoples. "It would be stupid for us to want to become a nation like any other— we are a special people, the Jewish soul was forged in a belly of fire."

Tagar, the German shepherd, has since retreated beneath the table and is dreaming of his quiet childhood in Russia—in the days before he was dragged off to Kirjat Arba near Hebron. Outside, the muezzin signals the call to evening prayer, and, within the walls of the house, you can hear the neighbors going about their usual business.

"We know why we're here," June says by way of farewell, "because in Hebron, God runs the show."

*Translated by Lilian M. Friedberg*

# 16

## TO EACH HIS OWN

One very normal morning of a very normal day in June 1998, Wendy Kloke looked out the window of her office on Potsdamer Platz–and gasped. On a billboard directly across from her, she read the slogan: "To Each His Own." "Has it really come back down to this?" Wendy Kloke, an American-born Berliner, asked herself. "Is it starting up all over again?" For at one time, the phrase *Jedem das Seine* had stood over the entrance to the Buchenwald concentration camp outside of Weimar. She needed to look a second time to grasp the situation: the Finnish firm Nokia was innocently advertising its new, colorful cellular phones. Every one should have his choice of colors. Hence, to each his own.

But Wendy Kloke, who works for the American Jewish Committee, considered the slogan taboo regardless of its purpose and turned to the media. The story hit the newspapers. Nokia pulled the ads, expressing sincerest regrets and replacing the slogan with a harmless quote from Shakespeare: "As You Like It."

At about the same time, the Anne Frank Center, a licensed affiliate of the Anne Frank House in Amsterdam, opened in downtown Berlin. According to a pamphlet, it "coordinates and facilitates the installation" of a traveling exhibit about

Anne Frank, "fosters the remembrance of National-Socialist crimes," and seeks to carry the "message" of Anne Frank's diary "into the present." This of course gave Berlin's senator for school, youth, and sports, Ingrid Stahmer, the occasion to say a few words of recognition at the opening.

Fifty-three years after Anne Frank was murdered in Bergen-Belsen, an educational group is using her as a stamp of approval. Today, thousands of Berliners would probably jump at the chance to take in the Jewish girl in order to express their aversion to National-Socialist crimes. But a few years ago, when a black African was beaten to death in Eberswalde, a half an hour's drive northeast of Berlin, not one of the city's good citizens came to his aid. And the inhabitants of the Dolgenbrodt community have even collectively decided to torch a home for asylum seekers in order to prevent any outsider from disturbing their idyllic village. In the meantime, a few areas of Brandenburg are now "foreigner-free zones," where foreigners are no longer tolerated.

Nowadays, symbolic antifascism enjoys high ratings in Germany: resistance against the Nazis becomes stronger as the Third Reich becomes more distant. But such exercises have nothing to do with present reality. Statistically, the new states are leading the pack in terms of xenophobic attacks, with Brandenburg in first place. Apparently a division of labor of sorts has developed. While some shout "Beware of the beginnings!" and "1933: Never again!" others shamelessly beat up everything that looks foreign—that is, everything that's not tall, shaved bald, or toting a beer bottle. When asked why adolescent thugs beat up everyone around them, social workers reply: because they've been robbed of their identity, because they're unemployed, because they don't know any better.

But when a few of these amateur thugs, euphemistically called hooligans, beat a French policeman unconscious at the World Cup, those same social workers fell silent, and Kohl declared the moral of the story. What happened in France brought "shame to Germany."

That means: when violent Germans mistreat foreigners on their own turf—that is to say at home games—you have to take into account their life circumstances as a mitigating factor. When they assault foreigners abroad, however, then they're acting like ordinary criminals who bring shame to Germany. They hurt Germany's image and threaten German exports.

There seems to be no remedy for perpetrators who commit violence for the sheer pleasure of it. Attempts to rehabilitate them are as ineffective as harsh sentences. Every society must contend with its own incorrigible dregs. But that fact can't let the thugs off the hook. Rather than practicing symbolic antifascism, getting angry about sentences like "to each his own," or marketing dead Anne Franks, concrete measures must be taken. For example, establishing a German foreign legion, so that they can wear themselves out somewhere else, rather than getting bored at home. Or banishing repeat offenders to a remote island, where there are no social workers and where they can bash in each other's skulls. That would take care of the antisocial dregs of society, and foreigners could move freely in Germany again without fearing for their lives, even in Dolgenbrodt and Eberswalde.

To each his own, then. It all depends on the context.

*Translated by Alexandra Parfitt*

# 17

## TO EACH HER MARKET VALUE

Some people spend their whole lives striving for fame; others manage to get it with one quick stroke. You can invent the whoopee cushion, box the current chancellor's ears, or win an essay contest about German history—just like Anna-Elisabeth (Anja) Rosmus from Passau. For years she has been inspiring headlines that strengthen her reputation as a terribly brave little girl while at the same time sending her hometown, Passau, into disrepute as a perpetual Nazi compost heap.

Born in 1960, the "disconcerting daughter of the city" (*taz*) grew up in solid surroundings: "I belong to the establishment by birth and by breeding." Her father was an active member of the right-wing CSU party, school principal, and chairman of the diocese council; her mother was a Sunday school teacher. Early on, she enjoyed the awareness of being different from the others. When her high school class was asked to elect a graduation speaker, she was astounded that "some raised their hands who didn't belong to the elite." She kept her natural lead over her peers by marrying her math teacher shortly after graduation. She married him "out of pity," because he had fallen hopelessly in love with her, and "to prevent any scandal," since her parents had already made all the wedding arrangements.

This act of mercy set the course. Anna-Elisabeth Rosmus, only twenty years old and recently married, sat at home and "was bored to tears." Then one day her father came over with an application for a student essay contest sponsored by the Körber Foundation in Hamburg: "My Hometown before the War." The honorary director of the contest was Karl Carstens, president at the time and himself a symbol of the prewar era in postwar Germany.

Killing time before matriculating at the university, Anna-Elisabeth Rosmus set off in search of documents and witnesses. Along the way, she got to know a city she'd never known. She stumbled onto a celebrated Heimatdichter, who called for a "de-Jewing" of Passau in 1919. She found out that the swastika flag had been consecrated in the Passau Cathedral as early as 1923. She discovered hymnals to the Führer in the *Passauer Bistumsblatt,* written by the bishop himself, who stayed on as editor-in-chief after the war and who was considered a member of the resistance. She met active local politicians who had collaborated with the Gestapo and yet others who covered for their friends. In short, she thrust into broad daylight a past that the city didn't want to know about. No wonder that the hard-working amateur encountered all possible obstacles in her path: the files she wanted to view were all recently checked out, confidential, or lost. She had to appeal to the constitutional court to gain full access to the city's archives.

But the effort paid off. Among over thirteen thousand contest participants, she took third place. Not bad for a twenty-one-year-old who, by the time she finished high school, didn't know that in 1944 the Allies "landed in Normandy in order to liberate Europe from National Socialism."

Surprised and encouraged by her own success, she expanded the prize-winning essay into a book: *Resistance and Persecution: Passau, 1933–1939.* A small Passau press published it in 1983 with an introduction by a former constitutional judge, Martin Hirsch. He praised the "thoroughness, technical knowledge, and democratic spirit" of the efforts to "make the crimes of my generation comprehensible." A year later, in 1984, Anna-Elisabeth Rosmus received the Geschwister Scholl Prize for the "naively purposeful, unbiased, and unrelenting perseverance . . . in pursuit of the truth." She appeared at the award ceremony nine months pregnant and escorted by her obstetrician. There, one publisher advised her to sign onto the Wort Literary Agency, which would "cash in royalty checks for me." One industry leader, who later died in a terrorist attack, worried about her safety: "He gave me tips about how I could protect myself by always driving a different route and leaving the house at different times each day."

By this time, Anna-Elisabeth Rosmus's fame had spread beyond the city limits. And she probably would have been satisfied with herself and her accomplishments if there hadn't been a pressing need that neither her husband nor the Wort Agency could fill: "I was twenty-four years old . . . and still hadn't ever had the opportunity to meet a Jew."

Since no one wanted to tell her how to "come in contact with a Jew," she leafed through the Passau telephone book, "but found no listings." Then she wrote a letter "to the chairman" of the Jewish Community in Munich, and the unexpected happened. He answered and invited Anna-Elisabeth Rosmus to a kosher meal. "I couldn't believe my luck: for the first time in my life I would meet a Jew!"

Anna-Elisabeth Rosmus experienced her first meeting with Hans Lamm, the president of the Jewish Community in Munich, much like an encounter with an alien in a remote parking lot for UFOs. "I didn't know how to conduct myself around him . . . I was excited, I was nervous . . . I didn't want to do anything wrong." But the plot continued just like in *E.T.* Anna-Elisabeth Rosmus and Hans Lamm became friends. Since he didn't have any children, he asked her to "give his name" to her first child—which she certainly would have done, if she hadn't had a girl. And when Hans Lamm died, then not only did she "feel the loss of a person," but she had to change her eating habits as well: "I lost my appetite at the sight of 'lamb' on a menu. . . ."

At this point, you'd think Anna-Elisabeth would have wondered if a sympathetic therapist and the five-volume 1927 *Encyclopedia Judaica* would have been more helpful than any more close encounters, which almost drove her over the edge. But it was too late for such a cost-benefit analysis. "A new world opened up which had been completely foreign to me." In the process, she met lots of people, whom she hadn't realized "even existed." Hanne Hiob, Bert Brecht's daughter, called her and invited her to participate in a program along with homosexual authors of children's books, lesbian pastors, and Sinti and Roma. Kurt Tucholsky's last significant other phoned from Sweden. She said: "I'm Gertrude, but just call me Topsy," sent her a message from Tucho ("He searched for people just like you in vain, he would have loved you"), and awarded her Tucholsky's death mask in "recognition of her fight against neofascism" in Bavaria, Germany, and the world. While the award-winning homewrecker collected material about the "Pogrom Night in and around Passau," it began to dawn on her "that this night was the 'prelude' to the Holocaust." Meanwhile, the director Michael Verhoeven was making a movie about *The Nasty Girl*. It won a Silver Bear at the 1990 Berlin Film Festival and was nominated for an Oscar in 1991, and it made its heroine famous in the United States. At the same time, the "indecent" movie posters were banned in the Passau area—yet another sign of the kind of harassment this professional taboo breaker had to wrangle with at home.

In a country where a few stupid city officials are able to create martyrs, it's only natural that the virtual resistance against the Nazis grows in proportion to the time elapsed between the present and the Third Reich. Not only is the current antifascist boom a bit belated, but its goal is inherently misguided. Whoever wants to succeed on this market must not only continuously perform good deeds and talk about them but also has to make sure that the production's details are just right. In 1991, Anna-Elisabeth Rosmus took both her daughters to Poland. "We went with friends . . . grilling and swimming, petting kittens and climbing trees, we visited the Auschwitz concentration camp memorial. . . ." Both girls rose to the occasion. They "plodded patiently from one concentration camp memorial to another, both compared and told me why they thought Treblinka was more impressive but why Auschwitz was more important."

Quite an accomplishment for two children, ages six and nine, at an age where one would really only expect them to explain the difference between a cookie and a candy bar. But Dolores Nadine and Salome Kassandra demonstrated, just like their mother, the appropriate attitude in every situation. If their teacher criticizes their poor handwriting, then one of the girls just might instruct him: "There are more important things in life than good handwriting. I was at an anti-Nazi demonstration yesterday." And when the entire three-person antifascist brigade visits a former concentration camp, you can be sure that the excursion ends with a heroic deed. For example, they rescued a four-legged camp resident named Misha. "Misha, the poor little devil, we brought him back from Auschwitz full of worms and fleas, starved to the bone." A poor dog from Altötting or Tauberbischofsheim wouldn't be half as much fun to show off.

But the brave-little-girl-staunchly-makes-her-own-way syndrome wouldn't be complete without admitting its dangers. There are people in this country, according to Anna-Elisabeth Rosmus, "who regret that I didn't live in the Middle Ages. . . . Then I'd have been drowned or burned at the stake. . . ." Even these people occasionally get ideas about how to shut up Joan of Arc's little sister. She reports numerous death threats and at least three attempts on her life. Once—on May 8—she was traveling by train. "Just outside of Nuremberg[!], neo-Nazi terrorists were waiting with large logs, which were thrown across the tracks." The train conductor noticed "the assassination attempt in good time" and brought the train to a halt at the last minute. While there were no signs to even indicate that neo-Nazi terrorists were at work or that she was the intended victim, after several years she is firmly convinced that she was the target, even if she admits: "Well, I ain't got no proof!" The other murder attempts, which she "just barely" escaped, were similar.

Since August 1994, Anna-Elisabeth Rosmus has been living with her two daughters and the dog she rescued from Auschwitz in Silver Spring, a suburb of Washington, D.C., "because I can learn so much more about the Holocaust while in the USA than I can at home in Lower Bavaria." After a year as a research associate for the Holocaust Museum in Washington, she is now researching independently "for one, two, three new books." For example, about the satellite concentration camp in Passau. Unlike the situation in Germany, in the United States "all the archives are open" to her, and there are "a bunch of concentration camp survivors" whom she can interview.

Anna-Elisabeth Rosmus, "a rather cheerful person with true Bavarian Gemütlichkeit" (*Stern*) is well adjusted to living abroad. That's primarily due to the fact that she has been heaped with prizes and honors. Happy to have finally found a genuinely good German who deserves their embrace, the Americans can't get enough of Anna-Elisabeth Rosmus. The aging "nasty girl" was a guest of honor at the opening of the Holocaust Museum in Washington and at the ten-year anniversary of the first Holocaust memorial in Detroit. She spoke at the opening of exhibits on Anne Frank, and she was the keynote speaker at a Kristallnacht memorial service at a large New York synagogue. In 1992 she was awarded the Holocaust Memorial Award in New York and two years later the Conscience-in-Media Award by the American Society of Journalists and Authors (ASJA). In Texas she was given the use of a "penthouse . . . suite in one of the ultramodern skyscrapers." Santa Cruz, California, declared an "Anna Rosmus Day." Barely having arrived in the United States, she "rushed from appointment to appointment, guest speaking at universities, benefits, and official meals with 'important' people." She flew "countless times every month to give speeches especially about Zivilcourage" and to hold "guest lectures about Passau and the Nazi era, about Germany and the neo-Nazis, about my work and its reception."

Meanwhile, she is approached again and again "in the elevator, on the subway, on the street, and in supermarkets." "Complete strangers" who recognize her from television trip "all over me" out of joy in "knowing that I'm here in their country."

But since even Anna-Elisabeth Rosmus can't be in more than one place at one time, and because the Shoah business is run with the same professionalism as the market for computer parts, the "currently most famous daughter of Passau" (*Münchner AZ*) is presently represented by two agents: one serves Jewish communities and human rights organizations, the other colleges and universities.

"My market value," Anna-Elisabeth Rosmus says with hip nonchalance "is estimated today at four thousand dollars per appearance, plus travel expenses." That market value "is related to my publicity" and climbs "the more you're in the headlines." Anyone who, like her, "has appeared on the CBS show '60 Minutes' has this market value." But four thousand dollars per appearance isn't all that much. As a survivor and Nobel laureate, Elie Wiesel's market value stands at twenty-five thousand dollars.

And while Anna-Elisabeth Rosmus didn't get one invitation to a single ceremony in Germany, she's constantly "invited to symposia and TV talk shows" in the United States. It doesn't bother her to be treated like "a kind of pillar saint," and only occasionally is she overcome by "a strange feeling, when people pay five thousand dollars to attend a benefit dinner in order to hear me talk about the Holocaust in my country." On such occasions, the incessant question about the meaning of the Holocaust surfaces from the recesses of history. The answer responds to the name of Anna-Elisabeth Rosmus.

In October 1996, the Jewish Community in Berlin awarded her the Heinz Galinski Prize, which comes with twenty-five thousand deutsche marks attached. According to the jury, she had "made a significant contribution to remembrance and explanation in spite of the greatest difficulties and circumstances."

Anja, the nice girl from Passau, was touched. She gave a few interviews and returned to the United States, where there is not only a demand for German villains but also a need, especially on the part of Jews, to occasionally meet a good German. Far away from Passau, she set herself to recycling her story one more time. In January 1999, a Hamburg PR agency revealed to the German media that Anna-Elisabeth Rosmus had struck again. "'The nasty girl' won't let up!" even "despite death threats and the most disgustingly insulting letters." Her newest book, slated to appear in March, "tells her own story of tough perseverance . . . and again makes public unbelievable revelations about Passau's Nazi past." She had used her stay in the United States and "the contact to the Jewish communities in order to work towards reconciliation."

She called her book *Out of Passau.* "Out of Her Mind" would have been more like it.

*Translated by Alexandra Parfitt*

# 18

## JUST IN TIME:
## A CATHOLIC CASUIST ON THE FRONT
## IN THE WAR ON TERROR

If there were a god in heaven and justice on earth, the world would have stopped for a moment on September 11, 2001. But since there is no god and no justice, all that changed was television programming, and the broadcast services just kept showing two commercial passenger planes approaching the towers of the World Trade Center, followed by the smoldering skyscrapers that soon collapsed like a house of cards. Everyone felt as though they were living a "nightmare" or the day after an "apocalypse"–no one wanted to believe what he'd just seen.

But even before the first of the dead had been recovered, the pop pundits were weighing in and speaking out to clearly identify the causes and warn us of the consequences. On Channel One, at a frequency of 88.8 on the FM dial, Berlin's SFB (Berlin's Free Broadcast Station) proceeded as usual with the show that airs every other Thursday at 10:30 P.M., "Late Night with Eugen Drewermann," starring Eugen Drewermann, the Catholic casuist and recusant from Paderborn who's been known to even butt heads with the Pope. Normally, Drewermann opens the show with a monologue about everything on God's green earth before he takes questions from listeners. This time, the attack on New York was the topic–why it happened and what "we" have to learn from it.

"We, too, are speechless. There is this horror that is without words, a grief that is beyond expression, a paralyzing sense of helplessness and dread in the face of the terrible abomination that descended upon unsuspecting, innocent people," the moderator said at the beginning of the broadcast, "and yet today more than ever, more than ever now in the face of this evil, we should grapple for words. In light of such a godless act, we want to address the question of God, the question of human nature. . . . Good evening, Herr Drewermann."

"Good evening, Herr Longard," the Catholic casuist answered and picked up where the moderator left off. "We are experiencing something that is utterly inhuman, and we are paralyzed by grief, horror, indignation, outrage, helplessness. . . . It's a terror of hitherto unprecedented dimension, of an unscrupulousness in action for which we really don't have the words."

Instead of succumbing to that very speechlessness, the Catholic casuist proceeded to talk about the "embargo policies against Iraq" and their consequences: "The United Nations estimates that about every month three thousand people die from the lack of basic food and supplies; within ten years, that will add up to the astronomical figure of one million human lives. . . ."

While it may seem rather callous in this context, I checked the math. If three thousand people a month die from lack of basic food and supplies, then that would be about thirty-six thousand a year, and in ten years, about 360,000– that's not exactly a million. A Catholic casuist needn't be able to add; presumably, what he was trying to say was this: if about as many people lose their lives in one terrorist attack on America as people in Iraq die every two months for lack of basic food and supplies, then the real problem is the lack of basic food and supplies in Iraq, not the terrorist attack in America.

At that point–it was still September 11–catch phrases like "nothing from nothing" and "you reap what you sow" hadn't yet been activated, but they were already looming like clouds on the horizon. The Catholic casuist then called to mind–for himself and his listeners alike–"Hiroshima, when, on the sixth of August, over one hundred thousand people were killed with a single bomb," and "Nagasaki, where, three days later, there were eighty thousand casualties in a single second, . . . with all their consequences. And obviously, we haven't learned a thing from these atrocities–quite the contrary, ever increasingly horrific, ever less scrupulous, the weapons ever more systematic, more barbaric, more atrocious, but all in the name of a putatively well-ordered state-sanctioned legitimation. . . ."

As surely as the Catholic casuist harangued anyone who would exercise violent force in the name of a "state-sanctioned legitimation," he demonstrated as much understanding for private killers acting of their own volition. "Terror is a surrogate voice for violence. Because legitimate concerns have gone unheard, it is the language of the powerless, the suicide bombers–it's just that it has escalated now; much in the same way the super powers engage in war, the political welterweights have obviously begun doing the same."

It certainly would have been a great comfort to the people who plunged to their deaths at the World Trade Center if, before the collision, they had been informed of the fact that someone whose legitimate concerns hadn't been heard was attempting to communicate with them in a surrogate voice for violence. The Catholic casuist assured us that this was the turning of "an endless screw, a millstone of blood whose ceaseless grind will not come to a halt unless we come to embrace the notion that security can only exist when we join forces in a brotherhood of man. And then we must do the seemingly unimaginable. We have to grasp the fact that behind this most horrific of things, there is something worthy of being heard–a concern, however perverse, however twisted, however inhumanely and cynically it seeks to impinge on normality. We have two thirds of the human race teetering on the brink of starvation and wondering how in the world anyone can glean any sense of security from the ongoing escalation of arms. . . ."

From this perspective, the attack on the World Trade Center could conceivably be viewed as a less-than-thought-out protest demonstration initiated by the organization "Bread for the World"–rather mean, but basically justifiable, if you think in the context of cause and effect.

"When we continue to perpetuate the causes of hate, of violence, of vengeance, we create a situation in which we, of course, become vulnerable. And will forever remain so. No one was prepared for this type of terror, . . . no one has ever acted in this manner before, it's a new dimension of military strategy among the world's welterweights . . . and we have to fear that this is just the beginning because we've already been engaged in building the military capacities of NATO's southern flank, especially against the Arab world. . . . We are preparing for the ultimate confrontation, in the name of civilization or the name of God. . . . The only salvation we might have would be if we were to comprehend that we're all in the same boat and that we can only achieve peace by coming together."

I turn the volume down on the radio, wondering who the hell condemned me to navigating the straits of history in the same boat as this Catholic casuist from Paderborn. Okay, so I'm among the guilty parties because I still have Anthon Berg chocolates and Icelandic salmon in the refrigerator–rather dubious predilections considering the starving masses in the Third World. On the other hand, I wasn't quite sure who had attacked whom and who'd leveled what: whether the ugly Americans had razed a couple of mosques in Mecca on behalf of Milky Way and Johnny Walker Red or terrorists had toppled two skyscrapers in New York in order to teach the uncivilized world a lesson. At this point, I thought, the moderator would have to intervene and clarify briefly. And indeed, Herr Longard broke in:

"The likelihood that a unanimous call for revenge and retaliation . . . will make itself heard is, of course, enormous. . . ."

I'm taken aback. Had a couple thousand people been murdered in one fell swoop at the central offices of Berlin's Free Broadcast Station, a unanimous call for revenge and retaliation would certainly not be heard, just a plea from the two surviving employees that we finally begin to understand that this type of terror as a military strategy on the part of the world's welterweights–an act of desperation whose causes must be sought in the broadcast schedule of SFB, which produces a new "Law and Order" series every couple of months while at the same time children in Rumania live on the streets. But the Catholic casuist, last seen on location in Iraq and Japan, had already gotten ahead of me and had now gone on to Palestine.

"One thing that really concerns me is that I'm afraid tomorrow's papers will be full of speculations about whether Palestinian terror can be suspected of having played a role in this. They'll parade before our eyes the way suicide bombers have been at work in Israel, on the West Bank, in the Gaza strip, and everyone will look for connections. . . . You have to take into account the fact that the Palestinians have instrumentalized terrorism as the ultimate expression of political discussions they have been denied, but what they are seeking is the establishment of their own state, which, sooner or later, cannot be denied them. The Israeli peace movement, Uri Avneri, and authors, important historians, think and speak the same way, but in order for that to happen, we need the influence of the United States of America. Many Palestinians hate the USA, but it's precisely because the Americans sit idly or half-heartedly by, watching the tragedy instead of acting as a committed world police force to do what Henry Kissinger's 'shuttle diplomacy' made possible between Egypt and Israel. Something like that is what's needed now–Colin Powell should go in there prepared to stay for four weeks or four months if need be, talking every hour of every day with alternating parties until peace has been reached, that would serve to finally defuse a significant force lurking in the background, above all in the Arab terrorist factions. . . . But to sit there with your hands in your lap simply in order to accommodate American domestic policy and watch things spiral out of control can't be the alternative."

Is there an inalienable human right to stupidity reserved for Catholic casuists or what? And what are the implications of issuing an errata before the error has even surfaced? No one but Paderborn's expert on surrogate voices for violence would have seen a connection between the Palestinians and these attacks. And no one but him would have had the hilarious idea of defining terror as "the ultimate expression of political discussions that have been denied." Especially not with regard to the Palestinian conflict, where terror has overshadowed political discussions between the Israelis and the Palestinians ever since the Oslo Accord in 1993, whereby terrorist acts are not designed to force peace but rather to hinder it.

But the Catholic casuist knows better, and he knows that the Palestinians hate the ugly Americans because they have neglected their duties as a world police force. And yet not a single "diplomat" has visited Washington as often as Yasir Arafat, and as recently as late 2000, at Camp David and Sharm el Shiek, Bill Clinton got down on his knees before Arafat in the attempt to persuade him to the historical compromise that Ehud Barak bit the bullet and agreed to.

The Catholic casuist's notions of "shuttle diplomacy" are about as lucid as his notions of the Israeli peace movement he refers to in the same way others invoke their "Jewish friends" before they go off on a tangent. And if Colin Powell doesn't drop everything for four weeks or four months or four years if necessary in order to conduct talks between the Israelis and Palestinians until peace has been reached, then the Catholic casuist won't hesitate to talk turkey at the next attack and scream "Go home!" at the top of his lungs.

"When we are hit, we feel humiliated. We're a long way from the times when Socrates could say in the fifth century B.C.: better to suffer injustice than to do it. And it's been two thousand years since Christ said, 'whosoever shall smite thee on the one cheek, turn to him the other,' and yet these lessons signaled the beginning of humanity. Even at the most archaic level, we feel humiliated when we are attacked and struck, when we've been injured, and then the cry for revenge still resounds. Precisely this is what we are hearing from George Bush today. 'We'll get 'em, dead or alive!' And I'm afraid that's just what will happen, the international systems of strangulation will be further intensified, especially with regard to the Arab states where the perpetrators are thought to be . . . the cries for justice will replace the call for revenge. In short, I'm afraid that precisely the consciousness that would be urgently needed, especially now in light of the horrific thing that has happened, is exactly what is being driven asunder as we fall back into the same old rut, and our suffering will once again only result in an escalation of our ability to inflict suffering, to achieve. . . . Somewhere there has to be a limit—there is not a single concept, not even of justice or of revenge, that should permit us to persist in this manner. Somewhere there has to be a point at which we all turn around. Today would be one such point."

What should George Bush have done in order to live up to the Catholic casuist's lofty expectations? Turn the other cheek like Jesus? Instead of mobilizing defenses, should he have instructed air traffic controllers to safely guide the next suicide bombers to their targets? Welcome to the USA! Be our guests! The Hancock Center is just eighty miles from here in light southwesterly winds! Or perhaps he should have crashed a couple commercial planes into residential areas as a sort of goodwill gesture toward all the underprivileged people who can't afford a one-way ticket to New York and Washington? Instead of turning around, the stubborn U.S. president persists and screams revenge while Osama bin Laden, acting on the Catholic casuist's advice, disseminates his declarations of peace worldwide.

After a brief musical interlude, someone calls in and says, "I think it's really too bad that people don't even begin to address the fundamental problem here. . . ."

"Right," the Catholic casuist responds, it even seems as though "we're planting some kind of Arab-phobia in our culture. Arab fundamentalism, Islam has become the latest entry in our glossary of threats. And everything we do in terms of building defense finds moral justification in this new perceived enemy. And as long as we keep talking about terrorism, our actions are completely legitimate . . . instead of taking the time and trouble of understanding how it came to this, that for entire populations, entire regions and cultures, terrorism has long since been seen as the surrogate voice for a political discourse that is long overdue."

There's a woman's voice on the phone saying she's "totally shocked," and the more she thinks about the attacks, the more she is reminded of the "surgical strikes" the Americans made "on Baghdad or Yugoslavia." She says she's afraid "that retaliatory strikes might already be made tonight in Kabul or somewhere." "We're completely shocked and would have gladly talked about it." It's probably "pretty cynical of me to say this," the woman says, but the Americans "are getting a little bit back," and if they "strike back tonight or whenever they do, they shouldn't be surprised when the whole thing just continues to escalate."

"The terrible thing about it is that this terror is basically a mirror image of the violence that has been carried out under state jurisdiction," the Catholic casuist voices his approval, and the woman agrees, "exactly." At which point the Catholic casuist takes another swing:

"Terror is the weapon of the powerless and is thus more indiscriminate, more unscrupulous, if you will. . . . When will we ever learn to see the language of hatred as a way of begging on bended knee for people to confront the reasons behind this deep-seated human despondency? There is no form of hatred, especially not between individuals, that is anything other than unrequited love.

Humans want to belong, that is the point behind all these maniacal acts. . . . They kill in order to be more involved. But who listens? In the Bible, God understands that and in the end spares Cain, but in human history, we simply continue to extirpate, we keep fighting evil basically by taking it to the next step in our own practices. We should get out of this vicious circle, and I can only wish that this day might bring the dawn of a new consciousness."

"Yeah, I wish it would too," says the woman who shares the Catholic casuist's view that the attacks on New York and Washington weren't only wakeup calls for the Americans but rather calls to all of us to accept mass murders as signs of unrequited love and to respond to them with love. How deeply the Nazis must have loved the Jews, how ardently must they have longed to be permitted a seat at the Sabbath table before they were shunned and forced to resort to maniacal acts. And yet, as always, whenever blood has been shed, there is hope "that this suffering will have at least served a purpose, otherwise it will just keep happening."

So it is that another day ends with a sense of purpose—ruins smoldering in New York and Drewermann fuming in Paderborn.

*Translated by Lilian M. Friedberg*

# Index

HENRYK BRODER was born in Poland in 1946, his parents having both survived German concentration camps. He began his career in journalism and continues to write, produce, and direct for German media.

SANDER L. GILMAN is Distinguished Professor of Liberal Arts and Sciences and of Medicine at the University of Illinois at Chicago. He is the author or editor of numerous books and articles, including *Jewries at the Frontier: Accommodation, Identify, Conflict* (coedited with Milton Shain).

LILIAN M. FRIEDBERG is assistant editor of the *German Quarterly* and a Ph.D. candidate in Germanic studies at the University of Illinois at Chicago. She has published articles in a variety of journals, including *New German Critique, Monatshefte,* and *American Indian Quarterly.* An award-winning translator (Kayden National Translation Prize, 2001), her translations have appeared in the *Denver Quarterly, Chicago Review, Transition,* and elsewhere.

Members of the Broder Translators' Collective include HUNTER BIVENS, a graduate student in the Department of Germanic Studies at the University of Chicago; CHRISTOPHER BRUMMER, who received his Ph.D. in Germanic studies from the University of Chicago in 2001; W. MARTIN, a translator and scholar currently living in Berlin; KENNETH MCGILL, a Ph.D. candidate in anthropology currently doing fieldwork in the former East Berlin; ALEXANDRA PARFITT, who received a B.A. in Germanic studies and comparative literature from the University of Chicago in 2002; ANDREA SCOTT, a graduate student in comparative literature at the University of Chicago and an associate editor for the *Chicago Review;* QINNA SHEN, who is working on a Ph.D. in German at Yale University; and KAREN WALTON, who is completing a master's degree in archives and records management at the University of Michigan and working in the Conservation Department at the Bentley Historical Library.

The University of Illinois Press
is a founding member of the
Association of American University Presses.

---

Composed in 9/13 Walbaum book
with Meta display
by Celia Shapland
for the University of Illinois Press
Designed by Copenhaver Cumpston
Manufactured by Thomson-Shore, Inc.


University of Illinois Press
1325 South Oak Street
Champaign, IL 61820-6903
www.press.uillinois.edu